Helga Thieroff

The Pain of Giftedness

Helga Thieroff

The Pain of Giftedness

My son who was different

LIT

This book is printed on acid-free paper.

Bibliographic information published by the Deutsche Nationalbibliothek
The Deutsche Nationalbibliothek lists this publication in the Deutsche Nationalbibliografie; detailed bibliographic data are available on the Internet at http://dnb.d-nb.de.

ISBN 978-3-643-91143-8 (pb)
ISBN 978-3-643-96143-3 (PDF)

A catalogue record for this book is available from the British Library.

Klosbachstr. 107
CH-8032 Zürich
Tel. +41 (0) 44-251 75 05
E-Mail: zuerich@lit-verlag.ch http://www.lit-verlag.ch

Distribution:

In the UK: Global Book Marketing, e-mail: mo@centralbooks.com
In North America: Independent Publishers Group, e-mail: orders@ipgbook.com
In Germany: LIT Verlag Fresnostr. 2, D-48159 Münster
Tel. +49 (0) 2 51-620 32 22, Fax +49 (0) 2 51-922 60 99, e-mail: vertrieb@lit-verlag.de
e-books are available at www.litwebshop.de

CONTENTS

Only those who think can experience life; it passes by the thoughtless
Marie von Ebner-Eschenbach (1830–1916), **Aphorisms**

Foreword

Trevor J. Tebbs PhD

PART ONE

After avidly reading Helga Thieroff's powerfully and painfully descriptive, yet clear-eyed biography, The pain of giftedness, to encapsulate the full scope of Helga's lovingly-written – and, I believe, important – essay in just a few words is a daunting task. The reader is compelled to accompany her, sympathize and empathize with her, as she makes her way bravely through the all too brief twenty-one years of Kai's life and beyond.

While Helga's journey begins joyfully with the birth of Kai, there is a swift shift in the nature of her responsibilities as a loving mother. She has to acknowledge Kai is different. Even at a very, very early age, he demonstrates both his intensity and ability, both of which are exceptional. She alludes frequently to her overwhelming realization of the astonishing degree to which Kai's nuanced social, emotional, and educational needs demanded attention not easily provided at home nor, in particular, provided in local schools.

Helga's account of her joys, trials and tribulations is riveting. Her determined acceptance of the daily demands is what I can only describe as courageous, inspiring. She and her husband are quick to learn about Kai's needs as his advanced cognitive development becomes more and more apparent via his unusual maturity of thought, reading ability, vocabulary and desire to learn, both at home and in various schools. In the circumstances, trying to find a "fit" for Kai was fraught not only with emotional stress, but also the stress caused by having to solve the practical necessities associated with supporting Kai's prodigious passion for learning.

I have no desire to rewrite Helga's story at this point, and so suffice to say the challenges briefly described above actually initiated some momentously visionary decision-making on her part. Namely, instead of giving up in a fit of despair, motivated by her love for Kai and her passion to provide for his learning needs, Helga established an educational program specifically designed not only to satisfy Kai and help him realize his potential, but also many other children besides.

PART TWO

This foreword is deliberately divided into two parts because while I found Helga's story invites me to share in her overall success, her cri de coeur also causes me to dig deep into my own psyche in the hope of discovering some rational and personal explanation for the utterly tragic event she later describes. While reading, questions constantly plagued my own mind:

"Why? Why? Why?" – a thoughtful, moving essay.

"What would I have done in the circumstances?"

"How would I handle the outcome?"

"How would any parent manage to stay so resolute?"

The story Helga tells is authentic. Not simply deeply personal and powerfully cathartic, but a story that needed to be written and, for a myriad reasons, deserved to be read. At a time when self-harm in young people and the issue of suicide are of global concern, her experience is particularly pertinent. The loss to humanity of so many young, bright-minded adults is a devastating scourge which forces heartbreak and suffering to enter the lives of families, friends, and communities large and small in every corner of the world.

Thinking back over the more than thirty years working with highly able young people and their parents, many come to mind. The opportunity to work closely with them and share a few moments of their lives, in the hope of contributing to their well-being, has always been a distinct privilege. While I never had the pleasure of meeting Kai, the detailed insights provided by Helga associated with the "ups and downs" experienced in his life resonate so accurately. Many stories could have been written – and can still be written – about the vulnerability of a worldwide population of highly able, intense, creative, sensitive, introspective and often lonely young people. Happily, some manage to discover who they are, what they can be and do, to find purpose and satisfaction in their lives. Others struggle to find a place, suffer for the wanting, but somehow find their way. Others, despite a huge capacity to do good in the world, compromised by a debilitating – and sadly common – amalgam of negative thinking, step away.

Knowing Helga, and having spent some hours in her company, I suspect she would not wish this piece to focus only on the sadness of her story. As authentic as the sadness is, her story also speaks of great courage and strength of character; not only her own but that of Kai. Helga showed grit and determination throughout Kai's life to make a difference, first in his life, but ultimately in the lives of hundreds of other young people whose needs had not previously been accommodated.

Not only do I account writing this foreword as a privilege, but also a responsibility I willingly accept. I invite the reader to take this book and – yes – share the sadness, but also consider ways we, our families, the society of which are part, can ensure valuable lives are not needlessly lost. It is my opinion that despite the love and caring attention so freely given by the parents of highly able individuals such as Kai, a paucity of knowledge about these young people, in combination with a poor understanding and support of their potential productivity, results in not only a heartrending depth of sadness but also a needless waste of a precious human resource for good.

Prologue

It was on an exceptionally sunny, mild day in December 2015 that I found it: a long-forgotten CD, which brought to life images from the past now that I held it in my hands again. I had been searching through my music collection for carols for the forthcoming Christmas service, when a CD with a self-designed cover suddenly caught my eye – dancing red letters on a white background: WITH LOVE ON MOTHER'S DAY. A flood of memories briefly took my breath away. I recognised the home-made CD: a Mother's Day present lovingly compiled by my son Kai, thirteen years old at the time – and who had died all of seven years before this day, having taken his own life at twenty-one.

My hands trembled when I inserted the CD into the player and pressed the start key. "Hello, dear Mama," the lively, light-hearted voice of my growing son rang out from the speaker, "with love on Mother's Day. I wish you happiness, good health and success, and much more. I've burned a CD for you. This CD has all the songs I could find about terrific mothers. I want to show you how much I love you. And I wish you a wonderful Mother's Day 2000. I hope I can make it even a bit more wonderful for you. From your Kai." This was followed by some moving songs, most of them in English. The lyrics included lines such as *Mama, oh I miss you sometimes, Mama, can you hear me when I cry* and *Mama, I love you.*

I remembered so clearly how touched I had been when I first played this CD fifteen years ago. What thirteen-year-old would have the imagination, or the courage, to surprise his mother with such a declaration of love? But even back then, I was already aware that my concerns about Kai's "different" intellectual and emotional nature were more than justified. Nevertheless, on that day in December I remained seated in front of the now silent player for a long time once the music had come to an end, giving free rein to my wildly reeling thoughts and emotions.

I could not sleep the following night. As images from Kai's life kept looming up in my mind's eye, I pondered the significance of finding this CD. I did not believe in spirit voices from the other world, but it almost seemed to me as if my deceased son wanted to say something to me again, perhaps for one last time. The following day I shared this experience with a colleague and asked her for advice. Under the impression of this conversation and my nightly broodings, I gradually began to realise something: I had to retrace my son's life story and record the experiences with his giftedness that we shared as a family!

Kai's life story is that of a young person with an exceptional intellectual giftedness and great emotional empathy. He was driven by a boundless love of freedom, forthrightly pursuing his own path and not shrinking back even from the ultimate consequence. I owe it above all to my son to publish this biography. But I also hope that by this means I can render support to all those who accompany highly gifted children and adolescents, whether as family members or in a professional capacity. With the background of my many years of professional experience, I would thus like to cast some light on what we went through with Kai, both from a personal and a theoretical perspective, in order to deepen an understanding of the typical character traits and frequent problems of highly gifted children and adolescents in our society. After all, giftedness poses extreme challenges to many of those affected and their relatives, and it will only be possible to improve the situation of these families with the support of a suitably sensitised society.

Unto us a special child was born

Kai saw the light of the world in the Maternity Clinic at Berlin-Neukölln on 12th January 1987. He was my first child, and no others were to follow. The delivery was carried out under the care of Professor Erich Saling, the renowned "father of perinatal medicine", whom I had sought out due to complications in my pregnancy. How happy I was to finally welcome my long-desired child after many weeks and months of waiting and a difficult birth! In the days after the delivery I held my son in my arms as often as I could and looked with delight at the small head covered in thin dark hair that stretched out towards me – and those deep-set, unfathomable eyes which would soon be scanning his surroundings with an inquisitive gaze.

Prof. Saling told me some days later that this behaviour was by no means normal for such a young baby. He closely observed my son and explained to me it was very unusual for a baby only a few days old to stare at objects and raise its head. He had never yet encountered such a child in his entire professional career. "Kai is a very special child," the professor assured me. Nobody at that time could have imagined just how accurate this assessment would turn out to be. In view of the complicated pregnancy and birth, Prof. Saling initially classified Kai as a risk child; this enabled us to benefit from a series of paediatric examinations in the Steglitz Clinic.

*

Once we had been discharged from the clinic and Kai had occupied his children's room in our home, we had announcements printed to spread the news of his birth to our families, friends and acquaintances. The front page was emblazoned with the lines with which we welcomed Kai to life on this earth, in cursive writing:

From deep repose sunken in self
I am awakened by the call of time
Light enshrouds me
Feelings remember
And proudly and freely consecrated to my very self
I am born into the world of humankind.
(Alexander Hans Gusovius)

When I read these lines today, I still feel the intensity of elation with which we celebrated Kai's arrival back then: the profound calm pervading the time before his birth was now dispelled, but what then followed was wonderful: Awakening! Light! Emotions! Freedom! A self! Finally arrived in the world of humankind! This poem was to tell little Kai how good it is to be here in this world, and that here is the place of individuality and freedom. And Kai understood us: he indeed developed a very strong sense of self-assurance and a distinctive desire for freedom at an extremely early age. Nevertheless, he also soon came to realise that the world of humankind was by no means only positive, but also had much abomination and hurtfulness to offer.

However, this was all still to come. In his first year of life, Kai was a contented child of sunny disposition, who delighted us with his rapid development. As a baby he loved being carried around to explore his surroundings, almost as if he had to remember all the details. He bypassed the crawling phase and already began to walk in his tenth month. At just under a year he started to speak. We were amused by his first words, which were not "Mama" and "Papa", but "on" and "off" when he worked the light switch. At this early age, Kai also started to understand the concept of quantity and developed his

Kai at his baptism, aged 10 months

own way of describing groups of similar objects: he designated *one* cup, *one* building block or *one* chair as "da"; *two* cups, *two* building blocks or *two* chairs as "dada"; and he referred to a larger number *of* similar objects as "dadadada".

*

Over the coming years, Kai conquered the world at breakneck speed. He showed little interest in conventional children's toys, but was enthusiastic about activities that were rather unusual for a child of his age. At the age of one he could be spellbound when playing with an egg whisk, at one and a half he was always keen to colour pasta in the kitchen under my supervision, and he loved to go to car parks with his father to identify the brands of the cars parked there. Kai was interested in all kinds of signs and symbols, and even before his second birthday he could already recognise all the most common makes of cars as well as the logos of banks and companies. A particular favourite of his were road signs, all of which he was already familiar with before his third birthday. I remember that we once even had to drive out into the country just so that Kai could see a "cow sign".

Shortly before his third birthday he used a kitchen towel to make a rubbish bin cover that would protect the lid of the "poor bin" from soiling. We collected empty toilet paper rolls and painted and processed them according to Kai's instructions. His imagination seemed inexhaustible, and we began to suspect that strenuous times were in store for us.

We only started to think of intellectual giftedness when Kai's language skills really exploded in his second year. Infantile babbling soon made way for comprehensible words, which he then pieced together to form simple and finally complex sentences. By the age of two, Kai was already using subordinate clauses, passive constructions and loanwords. I found it almost eerie to hear complex sentences from the mouth of a not yet two-year-old such as "I don't want to go to bed, because I'm not tired" or "I want to be pushed to the table."

But Kai surprised us time and again not only with his use of language. He already learnt to eat with a knife and fork at a very early age, and discarding the detested nappies was a pure act of will for him: at the age of two Kai decided he simply no longer needed them, and this met with success only a day later – he was "house-trained" once and for all. While Kai's rapid development filled us with joy, we also came to realise that his demanding behaviour, his stance of "further and further, more and more, constantly something new" was taking its toll on us. Kai needed only little sleep, so he often demanded my attention sixteen hours a day. When he was three years old, we had already gone through all the children's books from our shelves and the local libraries and had played all the audio and video cassettes, but Kai's hunger for more and more new "material" was boundless. In my desperation I often used to make up stories myself; Kai liked these the best of all anyway. If we ran out of "material", Kai – otherwise an endearing and well-balanced child – would lose his temper and I would have to search for new learning impulses for my insatiable son.

Things did not improve when Kai, now aged two and a half, launched into the endless loop of "why" questions so feared by parents. I was practically only there for Kai. Returning to my profession was out of the question – before Kai was born, I had been active at the university, where I had managed a facility for the integration of migrants and their children. Nevertheless, I was able to work freelance for a magazine in the evenings once I had put Kai to bed. This intensive time with our son gave me only little relief: while our relatives and friends were enthusiastic about our lovable, clever child, Kai simply exhausted them all. He loved to play shop with his grandmother, for example, but in such an intensive way that she could not bear it any more after two hours and deserted the field – or rather, the battlefield.

Unfortunately, in the first few years it was not possible for me to simply leave Kai with his grandmother for a weekend and recuperate: his grandparents lived far away and only seldom visited us, and our son was also very attached to his parents. Kai liked playing with his grandparents, but we parents always had to be nearby. The only person that Kai accepted without the presence of his parents was Bettina, a young woman we had hired for him as a mentor. During the precious hours that Kai spent in Bettina's care, I could allow myself a visit to the dentist or hairdresser. It was only after Kai started school that this extreme attachment subsided. His education in those early years was essentially left up to us parents: I provided his intellectual nourishment with books, while my husband's task was to introduce Kai to the world of car makes, signs and symbols. But since my husband had many professional commitments, it was mostly up to me to keep Kai occupied.

I was occasionally asked whether we did not want a little brother or sister for Kai. This question remained open for a while, but I must say that a second child would not have been at all possible for me in addition to Kai – I would not have been able to find either the necessary time or the energy.

What made life a little easier for me at that time was Kai's attitude towards rules: he followed them willingly. If we told him for example that he should not go near the power sockets, he kept away from them and we could be sure that he would not touch them in future either. He was always very careful with knives after we once told him they were sharp and could hurt him. In this regard, Kai's upbringing was not very difficult for us. We were thankful for this, because on the other hand his boisterous striving for self-determination placed great demands on us.

*

Before Kai's second birthday, we were wondering whether our child, who had such a thirst for knowledge and was so far in advance of his age, should not perhaps now go to kindergarten. Kai was familiar with kindergartens from our extensive walks. Whenever we went past one, he intently watched the playing children and often expressed a desire to go there too. On the occasion of a risk assessment examination in the Steglitz Clinic I therefore asked the paediatrician whether she would find it appropriate for us to register Kai for kindergarten. As if at pains to demonstrate his aptitude for kindergarten, our not quite two-year-old son excelled during the examination with statements such as "I don't want the scissors with the rounded tip; I'd rather have the scissors with the pointed tip!" The doctor was astonished but nevertheless warned us against having Kai enrolled. She perceived that he was not only a highly gifted child, but also an extremely sensitive one who would have difficulties among large, noisy groups of children. This appointment was our last examination at the Steglitz Clinic. Since Kai's development by far surpassed all expectations, the paediatrician no longer saw any reason to treat him as a risk child.

However, we did not heed her advice against registering Kai for kindergarten. As my two-year-old regularly demanded the utmost from me and I often had the feeling I could not offer him enough, I decided to try enrolling him despite this medical advice. Of course, this did not turn out well and I found myself picking up a screaming child from the kindergarten day after day. When the teacher told me that Kai had the most difficulties of all children in adapting to the daily routine, I decided to put an end to this experiment and look for a different educational opportunity for him. But I did not know what this could be, because one thing had now become clear to me: conventional education and support were simply ineffective with Kai. So I decided to busy myself with my son as best I could at home again. Through my circle of friends I tried to give Kai as much contact as possible with other children and made sure that he had enough physical exercise in the form of regular walks, and later also with children's swimming classes and with bicycle and scooter riding.

When we suddenly noticed around the time of Kai's second birthday that he knew all the letters of the alphabet – the capitals and the small letters, without our having explicitly taught them to him – we were certain that Kai was intellectually gifted. In my search for appropriate information I contacted the German Society for Highly Gifted Children (Deutsche Gesellschaft für das Hochbegabte Kind e.V. – DGhK), without suspecting that this telephone call would change my professional life.

We launch the "Children's Club"

The German Society for Highly Gifted Children was established in 1978, at a time when the topics of giftedness and associated educational grants still had nothing of today's relevance within society. Even twelve years later, when I tried to adapt to living with a gifted child, in conversations with acquaintances I noticed that "giftedness" was still an unfamiliar concept to many people. But to be honest, I had hardly concerned myself with this subject either until that time. Before Kai's birth, during my pregnancy, it had simply not occurred to me that my child could be exceptionally gifted. I had not been expecting this, and it was not important to me how intelligent my child would turn out to be. On the contrary, my husband and I had agreed that we would lovingly welcome any child – even if it were handicapped – and care for it according to its needs. When we learnt that Kai was gifted, I often wondered what sinuous quirk of fate – or of heredity – had bestowed such a special child on us, of all people. We, his parents, were academics and my husband had already embarked on a university career and had striven for a professorship, but this alone could not be the explanation. Giftedness had never been a matter for discussion in our family environment either.

More recent intelligence research has found some answers to the origin of giftedness – and also put into question a popular myth surrounding this topic. Among the general public, giftedness in children is seen above all in connection with fathers, or with male family members in general, especially since in many families they are seen as the "clever" ones. According to current research, however, men apparently play a rather subordinate role in transmitting intelligence to their children. This assumption is based on the fact that many of the genes influencing the development of intelligence lie on the X chromosome. Men, who of course only have one X chromosome, transmit this – and the "intelligence genes" it contains – to their daughters, not but to their sons. Boys inherit the X-chromosomal genes for intelligence exclusively from their mothers. But it is also a fact that both high and low intelligence are found more frequently in men than in women.[1]

There are apparently not only genetic, but also cerebro-physiological differences between people of high and average intelligence. The general assumption is that all forms of giftedness have a biological basis. Just as it is undisputed that retarded intellectual development has a cerebro-physiological cause, it is assumed that the same applies to giftedness. It has been established that no amount of specific intellectual activity can elevate a person of average intelligence to the level of a "child prodigy". Rather, gifted people appear to have "differently functioning" brains.[2]

---

1 Eggers C. Störungen der Intelligenz, in: Rohde A., Marneros A. (eds.), Geschlechtsspezifische Psychiatrie und Psychotherapie. W. Kohlhammer 2007

2 Winner E. Hochbegabt – Mythen und Realitäten von außergewöhnlichen Kindern, Klett-Cotta 1996

Nevertheless, the personal environment also appears to significantly influence one's degree of giftedness. The contribution of environmental factors to differences in intelligence between individuals is estimated at 40 to 50 per cent. According to the current state of knowledge, the environment has a formative influence on intelligence especially during childhood and early adolescence. These effects seem to diminish with increasing age, however, and genetic factors then play a more predominant role. Complex interactions thus constantly occur between hereditary factors and the environment over the course of one's life: on the one hand, the intelligence genes determine a child's behaviour – and the environment reacts accordingly. But on the other hand, these hereditary factors can have quite different effects depending on the environmental influences to which they are exposed. When the environment offers comparable opportunities for development, differences in intelligence can then more plausibly be explained by genetics. Under different conditions for development, however, the environment is thought to play a much more significant role.[3]

*

Of course, I did not yet know any of this two and a half years after Kai's birth, when I turned to the DGhK in search of advice. I had a long conversation with the director at the time, a professor of primary school pedagogy. I learnt a great deal from her about the special needs of intellectually gifted children, but at the same time I also

3 www.karg-stiftung.de

heard that no promotion programmes were yet available for gifted preschool children. I was somewhat astonished by this: since it was only natural and appropriate to provide learning offers for children with retarded development, I would have expected the same for children at the other end of the scale.

After this conversation I felt greatly disappointed at first. I had understood that at least up to the time of my son's enrolment in primary school, I was left to my own devices in catering to his special needs. On the other hand, it was clear to me that it was out of the question for Kai to attend a conventional kindergarten. Time and again, I had seen that in his interactions with children from our neighbourhood and our circle of friends, Kai felt somewhat left out in the company of children of his own age or slightly older. As a two-and-a-half-year-old, he felt most at ease in the company of children aged five to eight. However, it was not only Kai's intelligence that gave me cause for concern when it came to attending kindergarten, but also his extremely sensitive nature. Kai treated other children very affectionately and could not stand aggression at all. He would definitely have felt out of place in a large, at times wild group of children.

In connection with aggression among children, I remember a further telling episode. We were once visited by a boy who was noted for his somewhat wild, impulsive style of playing. But on that day, all was peaceful and harmonious, without the usual pushing and shoving. Kai, now two years old, drew his own conclusions from this new situation. After his visitor's departure he proclaimed, "Dennis came today purely out of interest. He didn't push me!" Once again, I was astonished not only at my two-year-old's eloquence but also at his distinctive capacity for empathy.

All in all, I was convinced that my son required individual support – and this was exactly what a regular kindergarten could not offer. In the course of my preoccupation with the phenomenon of giftedness, it was only much later that I encountered an excellent assessment of intellectually gifted children by the Canadian researcher Dr. Michael M. Piechowski, who sets out why these children often assume the role of an outsider in groups such as kindergarten or school classes. Piechowski writes:

"What is Normal?

"Gifted children are highly stimulated by what's going on around them, and by what moves them from within their being. Because they can be so greatly stimulated, and because they perceive and process things differently, gifted children are often misunderstood. What is normal to them is not perceived as normal by others. Their excitement is viewed as excessive, their high energy as hyperactivity, their persistence as nagging, their questioning as undermining authority, their imagination as not paying attention, their persistence as being disruptive, their strong emotions and sensitivity as immaturity, their creativity and self-directedness as oppositional disorder. The more gifted they are the farther they stand out from the norm." [4]

This description precisely fits Kai, just as he was – or was perceived – in his childhood.

*

While I was trying to come to terms with the lack of adequate sup-

4 Piechowski MM (2010) Ein Vogel, der zur Sonne emporsteigen kann: Erhöhte Sensitivität der Begabten. Journal für Begabtenförderung. 2:7-21

port opportunities for my son, a solution occurred to me: I could put my educational and psychological qualifications to use and establish a support group for gifted children myself! In this way I could kill two birds with one stone: Kai would receive adequate support, and I could extend my scope of professional activity.

I soon developed a concept for the "Children's Club", which was to be initiated as an offer from the DGhK. We launched the club in early 1990, when Kai turned three years old. In our brochures for interested parents, it was important to us to point out that need-oriented support for gifted children was not a "circus act". How often are the parents of gifted children accused of subjecting them to precisely this sort of "drill"! I myself have hardly ever experienced such hostilities born of envy and incomprehension, since right from the outset – from the time I first noticed Kai did not get on well with children of his age – I avoided children's groups and other regular mother-and-child encounters. Other mothers who brought their gifted children to the Children's Club had already gone through some painful experiences. These parents often react with complete withdrawal: they avoid supporting their smart offspring at all – after all, their children must not become outcasts! But this very reaction is calamitous: children who are constantly underchallenged are bound to develop behavioural disorders.

It is not enough to simply reassure a demanding child brimming with unanswered questions that he or she will be able to go to school one day. The right time to address a topic comes when a child asks questions of its own initiative – even if this seems to be very early. A comparison with other children is of no help in such situations. My son showed me quite clearly that ignoring a gifted child's inexhaustible thirst for knowledge is not an option: whenever there was nothing that could hold his interest, my otherwise cheerful child would quickly turn into a little pest.

For the Children's Club we employed two assistants, who were to provide support for the children together with me as director, and we waited for the first registrations. These were not long in coming: the demand far exceeded our expectations, and we saw this as confirmation that there was an urgent, widespread need for support offers for gifted children. The enormity of this demand was also borne out by the fact that we were even contacted by families from distant regions. We started our courses with five children aged three to four, who came to us several times a week; the group rapidly grew to around twenty. Kai himself attended the Children's Club up until his enrolment in primary school at the age of five.

Our idea was to provide gifted children with individual, holistic support in a wide variety of areas – from the natural sciences and the world of letters and numbers to foreign languages, theatre, art and handiwork. We sowed seeds and planted flowers, talked about temperature and water, combinations of colour and environmental protection, made finger puppets, board games, Mother's Day presents and geometric solids, discussed traffic and transport, cooked and baked, and undertook experiments in photography in the darkroom. There was also no lack of excursions: we visited the zoo, the museum and the aquarium; we often went to the theatre and paid visits to workshops, a hospital and a dental practice. We regularly staged game afternoons and picnics, along with spontaneous get-togethers at the children's own homes. At the game afternoons, the children played with such imagination that they neither missed nor needed adult supervision.

This was a very intensive, but also encouraging time, and our commitment had certainly paid off: the children felt at ease and had companions to talk to. At the Children's Club, most of them for the first time had the important experience of being accepted with their exceptional giftedness. This helped them to reinforce their self-esteem and to gain confidence in their special abilities, which normally only met with resistance in the "outside" world. From my professional standpoint, I can by no means confirm the commonly held view

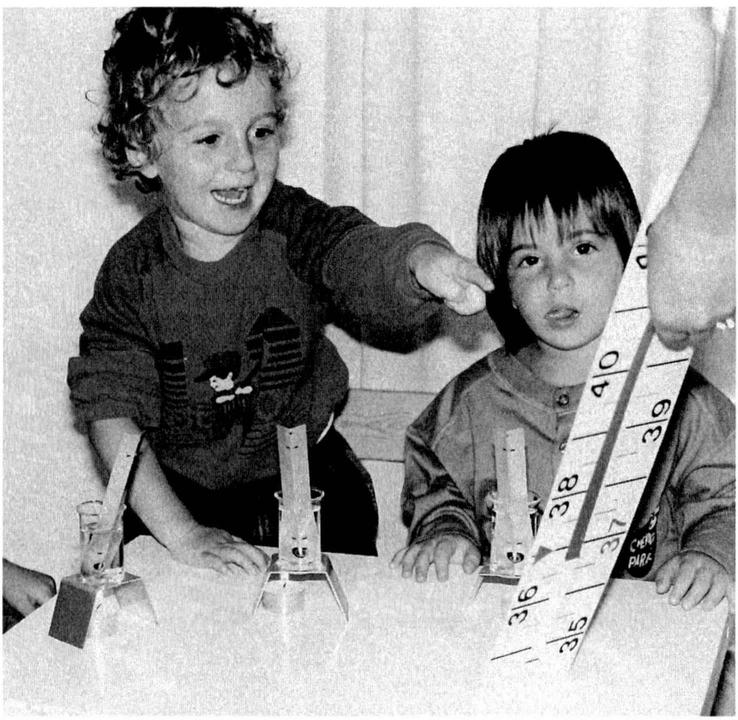

Kai (left) as a three-year-old, experimenting at the Children's Club

that intellectually gifted children in particular need to learn social behaviour. Even at a very young age, gifted children are not concerned with showing other children that they are "better" or know more. They simply want to formulate their thoughts, find answers, recognise rules and make these known. But this very behaviour is often seen as "smart-alec" and antisocial.

For Kai too, it was a liberating experience to be able to communicate at eye level with children of his own age at the Children's Club. Whereas he had previously only ever sought contact to much older children, he now for the first time found good, close friends of the same age and really started to flourish. His friends were important to him, and he resolutely stood up for them whenever he found it necessary.

When I think back today to our time at the Children's Club, I see Kai as a three-year-old in my mind's eye – with his slim figure, which had only just grown out of his "baby fat", and his dashing curly blond hair. I see him sitting at the table with the other children, listening with interest, and jumping up enthusiastically time and again to explain or comment on something or other; but above all I see his eyes, gleaming with intelligence and a thirst for knowledge, which lit up his entire eager little face. I know today that we were in our prime during the years at the Children's Club, and I often wistfully think back to this time.

*

Kai's first attempts at reading and his first spontaneous forays into writing also came about during this intensive time of bubbling creativity. He knew already all the letters of the alphabet before his second birthday, but we consciously avoided promoting his reading skills: we did not want our child to "fall out of line" any more than he already did! Rather, we waited for him to discover reading on his own initiative; and so it came about just after he had turned three. I remember one evening when Kai – already lying in bed in pyjamas, playing with his teddy bear – suddenly called out "Ass Y! Ass Y!" and proudly added, "I can read now, Mama!" I was bewildered at first and did not know what he was talking about, but my son then showed me his teddy's brand label with the name ASSY. He had actually managed to join the letters together to form a word! I explained to him that the Y is pronounced as IE when it is part of a word, because he had no way of knowing this yet. Kai's reading skills rapidly developed from that day onward, and by the time he started school he could already read and understand long, unfamiliar texts and books.

Also when he was three, Kai started to add comments to his always highly imaginative and detailed drawings, and to give them titles. This was not merely copying, memorising and then reproducing words, as can usually be seen with preschool children who write their names or simple words. Rather, Kai was already able to write down a word that he had heard or thought of. His drawings were resplendent with words – of course not always correctly spelt – such as traffic lights, car, lollipop man, checkmate and various animal names. It was not long before he wrote his first short stories.

During his years at the Children's Club Kai was noted for his astonishing linguistic fluency, which increasingly demonstrated his ability to accurately group together perceptions from highly diverse fields of experience. Many comments by my three-year-old son make me smile even today in view of their astuteness. In my notes I find sentences like these:

The magician is dead. But perhaps he will rise from the dead like Jesus Christ, and Caspar will be in danger again.

Why don't we have to pay for presents?

Walking is somewhat like running, but not fast, just slowly.

In an aeroplane: *Look – the world looks like a map now.*

Lollipop man. A drawing with a spontaneous attempt at writing by Kai, aged 3

The following story also illustrates Kai's astonishing associative capacity. One time when we were on holiday, two acquaintances offered to take our three-and-a-half-year-old for a walk. He was reluctant, so I delved into my box of tricks and turned the walk into an expedition to buy an ice cream. "You only want to entice me," Kai then proclaimed. Our acquaintances fell silent. The woman from the next table asked, "Do you really know what 'entice' means?" She promptly heard the answer: "It's like with Hansel and Gretel. The witch enticed the children in that story too." This was just one of many times we came to realise that tried-and-tested "enticements" simply proved ineffective with our smart son.

We were also astonished to learn at what an early age Kai knew that statements should not always be taken literally. The three of us

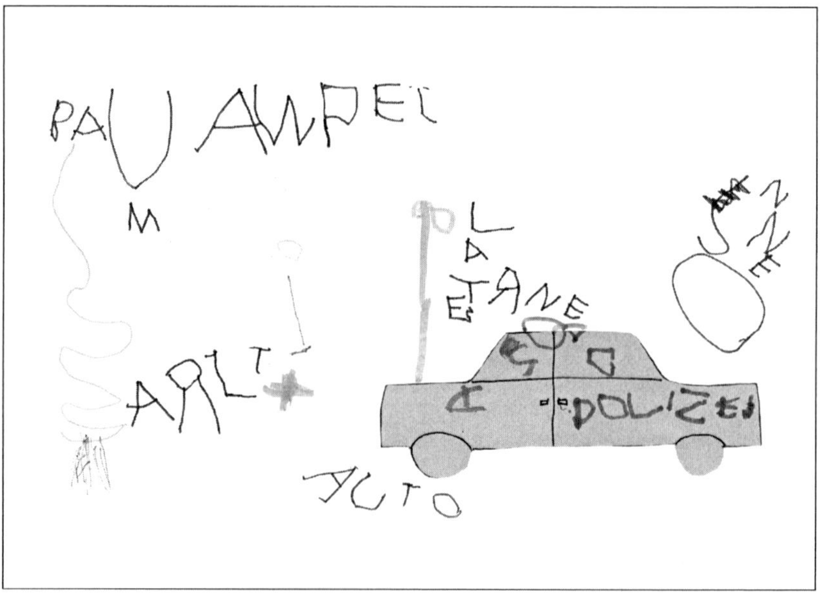

A stencilled car with dictated text. A drawing by Kai at the age of 3

Annotated animal collage by Kai at the age of 3½

Beginning of a short story that Kai wrote by himself at the age of 4 *(This book is about a dog. Once upon a time there was a dog. It had a red bow.)*

were sitting and talking one evening in our living room. When my husband commented on something unpleasant, that I can no longer remember, with the sarcastic remark "Well, isn't that just great", Kai looked at him sceptically and asked, "Papa, did you mean that sarcastically?" To this day I do not know where he picked up this word, which is not a normal part of a three-year-old's vocabulary.

*

A further highlight of Kai's childhood was his birthdays. In the days of the Children's Club, when Kai turned four and then five, we staged small birthday parties that he was allowed to manage himself. He greatly enjoyed this. Kai chose his guests – friends from the Children's Club and children from our circle of friends – created invitation cards and planned the games for the party. While Kai was otherwise rather restrained and by no means domineering in his interactions with other children, it was very important for him to be in charge on these occasions. At one of these parties, for example, he hit on the idea of making headbands together with his guests. He self-confidently assigned me the task of buying the ribbons for these, along with glitter for decoration. I was astonished time and again at my son's inventiveness, and I gladly assisted him in his preparations.

I was amused by Kai's unusual, at times whimsical birthday wishes. While other boys aged four or five normally ask for Playmobil, Lego or action figures, Kai's interests were quite different. For his fifth birthday, for instance, he wanted a refrigerator for his room because he wanted to cool and open his drink bottles and cans in his own domain. And so it came about that at the age of five he was given a small refrigerator of his own – along with the long-desired towels embroidered with his name.

Kai planned his birthday parties far in advance. Long before his fifth birthday, for example, he wanted to invite a friend from the Children's Club who was not allowed to celebrate birthdays, as he was from a family of Jehovah's Witnesses. Kai thought the matter over for a while and finally came up with a solution to this dilemma that astonished us in view of its maturity. Without further ado he set a different date for the celebration – three months before the actual

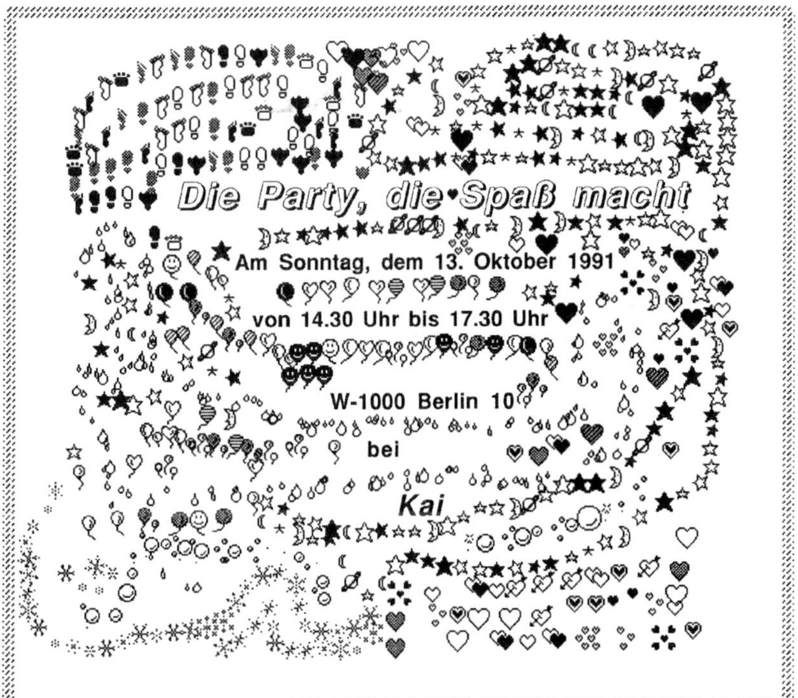

Invitation to a party, created largely autonomously on computer by Kai, aged 4½

day. As this was now no longer a birthday party, it was no problem for his friend to join in. I still remember how Kai had insisted on designing the invitations for this party himself on the computer. This of course was at a time when it was by no means usual for children of his age to operate a computer. Since my husband worked at the university, we already had a computer at home at an early stage, later also with Internet access; our son naturally did not let the opportunity slip by to explore the secrets of this device too. So at just under five years of age, he was well able to use a design programme at an elementary level. I have kept a printout of this invitation all these years. It is a firework display of dancing hearts and stars, interspersed with a simple but promising invitation text: *The fun party.* Under this – inserted with our help – were the date, time, address, and then on the very last line the name of the proud host: *at Kai's place.* On that afternoon too, Kai took it upon himself to entertain his own guests.

All in all, during those years I had managed to provide my special little son with an environment in which he felt at ease and seemed contented. This made me happy, and I looked to the future with confidence.

*

Kai turned five in January 1992. We parents agreed that he should be registered for school the following autumn, since we could not have imagined keeping him away for school for another whole year. But in view of the legal situation at that time, we did not know how we could have our son enrolled at a primary school at the age of five. A fortuitous quirk of fate then came to our aid: my husband was offered a university tenure in Norway, and we heard that an early enrolment for primary school was possible there under certain conditions. So we left our familiar surroundings in Berlin and moved to Oslo. Kai's enrolment at primary school opened up a new chapter in his life story – a chapter that I would dearly like to rewrite if only I could.

Kai's first school years in Oslo and Berlin

Kai's schooldays started at the German School in Oslo in August 1992, at the age of five and a half. This early admission was subject to a condition: we had to demonstrate our son's suitability to attend school in an aptitude test – the so-called "intelligence test". Before moving to Norway, we therefore subjected Kai to an IQ test at the University of Tübingen, in the knowledge that an intelligence test for a child at such a young age is only of limited informative value: it neither provides a finely differentiated picture of giftedness, nor does it allow conclusions to be drawn regarding the IQ level that can be reached in later years. On the other hand, a well-conducted test can be more or less informative, and this was sufficient for our purpose.

The IQ test at the University of Tübingen attested Kai a high level of general intellectual giftedness. Although this result did not surprise us, we now for the first time had sound evidence of our son's unusual intellectual capacity. It was only several years later, when Kai was tested for a second time, that we learnt just what dizzying heights Kai's IQ had in fact reached.

For the time being, however, Kai's first day at school was looming up in front of us: while I looked forward to it, I also felt some apprehension. I do not remember Kai's first day at primary school in Oslo very well. In my search for mementos of that day I came across a photo in my album that must have been taken at the enrolment ceremony in the school hall. A row of school beginners – boys and girls – can be seen on the stage, clutching their traditional enormous cornets full of sweets, with a blend of pride and foreboding on their faces. I discovered Kai with his curly hair at the right of the picture. His face was turned away from the camera, so I could not interpret his expression. However, I could clearly see that my son was by far the smallest child in the row – a delicate toddler holding a cornet that was far too big for him.

Kai settled down well in school despite his young age. The classes were small, and there were differentiated learning offers well matched to the individual pupils' level of aptitude as well as activities involving several classes. Kai liked school so much that we also registered him for the after-school activities, where he baked biscuits, sang and played together with the other children in the afternoon. During school holidays and at weekends we went on walks or collected mushrooms in the surrounding woods, which we then used at home to cook some delicious dishes, and we often went skiing in the winter. I myself found these undertakings very enriching, and Kai also enjoyed them. He also discovered a passion for riding on public transport in Oslo. We travelled by train whenever the opportunity arose, and it was not long before Kai could recite all the stations by heart in the correct order.

*

The idyllic life close to nature that we had enjoyed in Norway came to an abrupt end when my husband's tenure at the University of Oslo expired in January 1993. After a six-month sojourn in Norway we returned to Berlin, where we registered Kai – who was now six years old and therefore eligible to start school in Germany – at the local primary school. This was a large school with many classes and a big, complex playground. I anxiously wondered whether all would turn out well.

Already on the first day, when I went to pick up my son his teacher greeted me in a state of alarm. She was at a loss about what to do with Kai, since he already knew everything and was far ahead of the other children. She suggested I should allow him to skip a class. But I knew for certain that this was not what I wanted. How should my son, who already now was younger than his classmates, keep up with second-graders in his emotional and motoric competence? I declined his teacher's suggestion and decided to wait and see how things would develop.

However, I did not have the chance to wait for long. When I went to the school playground during the break on the second day to see how Kai was faring, I was confronted with a sight that filled me with concern and forced me to take immediate action. First of all, I searched the playground in vain for my son. And then I saw him: Kai was standing alone in the midst of the noisily playing children. He had his hands pressed firmly to his ears, and as I came closer I could hear that he was singing loudly to drown out the noise of the playground. It seemed to me as if Kai wanted to spin a cocoon around himself with the sound of his own voice, to protect himself against the thunderous din that was overwhelming him.

One could smile at my son's excessive sensitivity to noise and see this as an "oversensitive" reaction by conventional standards, but I sensed that there was more to this matter and I definitely had to take it seriously. It was only several years later, in the course of my preoccupation with giftedness, that I came across the personality theory of the Polish psychiatrist Kazimierz Dabrowski[5], which provides a well-founded explanation of this episode and many other puzzling behavioural traits of my son.

In his personality theory, Dabrowski identifies a highly sensitive nature as a salient feature of giftedness. He distinguishes five forms of high sensitivity, each of which he considers to be innate – psychomotoric, sensory, intellectual, imaginative and emotional sensitivity. These variants are differently manifested among individuals and are not only found in gifted people. But the more forms of high sensitivity that are robustly manifest in a particular person, the more readily one can describe this person as highly sensitive. High sensitivity alone does not amount to giftedness, although it is an important prerequisite. As Dabrowski states, a person can be highly sensitive without being gifted, but giftedness is not possible without a high degree of sensitivity.

I see the playground episode as a clear indication of Kai's distinctive sensory faculty – his ability to react to stimuli from his surroundings with very strong emotions. People with this capacity can be overjoyed by pictures, music or odours, but they can also experience "trifling" matters such as a stocking seam, a clothing label or

5 Dabrowski K (1996) Multilevelness of emotional and instinctive functions. Part 1: Theory and description of levels and behaviour. Lublin, Poland: Towarzystwo Naukowe Katolickiego Uniwersytetu Lubelskiego

everyday sounds in their surroundings as unbearable. Throughout his childhood, Kai showed us time and again how much he disliked loud environments, so I was not at all surprised that he suffered tremendously from the clamour in the school playground; on the other hand, I had been unaware that this too was a facet of his giftedness.

I reacted to the playground incident by immediately removing my son from the school.

*

We set out in search of a smaller, quieter school that could better cater to children's individual needs; we finally decided in favour of a sports school with a more favourable building layout and a lower overall noise level. Additional sport lessons were offered, and there

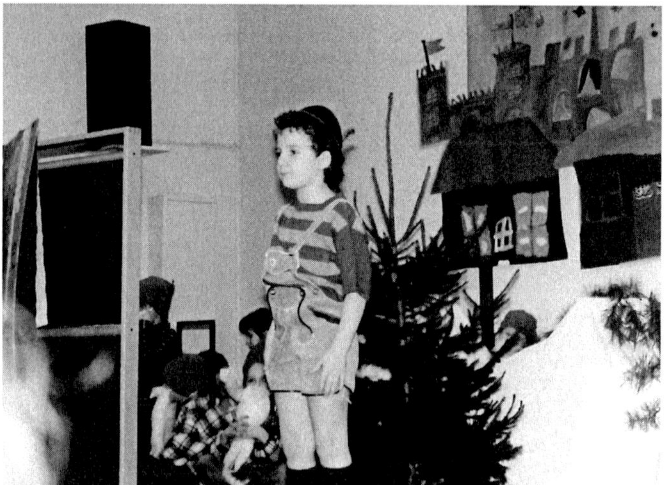

Kai at a school play in second grade

were many theatre projects, which Kai greatly enjoyed. At the school functions he recited poems from the third-grade syllabus and acted in long plays. He mastered all his performances with bravura.

A particular highlight was a visit from a television team that was looking for children to appear in a programme called "Dingsda" (Thingamajig). Kai was overjoyed at being selected to participate in the shooting session along with some other children. Their task was to paraphrase given words in a series of brief scenes filmed at the school. These scenes were then replayed during the live programme, and two celebrity couples competing against each other had to guess the original words. On the evening when Kai's episode was broadcast, we all assembled in front of the television set and enjoyed our son's first media appearance.

*

Kai effortlessly mastered the demands of his first school year. It gladdened my heart to read in his first-grade report that despite his young age, my son fulfilled all the various requirements of his schooling with great success. This handwritten report, which I have kept along with other documents from Kai's life, tells of his more than satisfactory performance at school:

"Kai is a highly imaginative, intelligent child. He has an extensive vocabulary, can argue very well, and understands puns und makes up his own. He is superior to his classmates in his language skills. Kai can read and immediately comprehend any text without help. Arithmetic too is no problem to him, since he can think logically and work systematically. Kai is sometimes still rather slow in

solving written tasks. Although he is younger than his classmates, he does his best to be just as skilful and fast as the others in sport. Kai's drawings are highly imaginative and rich in details, but often require interpretation. He can handle conflicts very well. Kai is a happy child who is willing to compromise."

In retrospect I can say that the year and a half which Kai spent at the sports school in Berlin were not a bad time for him. We were fortunate that the headmaster was at pains to provide finely differentiated support for the individual children. He had intended to establish working groups, for example, which the children could attend

Kai as a second-grader

as they felt inclined. Unfortunately, however, the government education authority did not approve this project.

One factor that Kai found very difficult in his early days at primary school – and which not even the headmaster with his progressive approach could change – was the syllabus, which my son could not evade. When the children were repeatedly given the homework assignment of writing pages full of the letters E and I, my son went into a rage and at times even threw his schoolbooks into the corner. As he could already write at the age of three, he could see no sense in such exercises. So I was all the more surprised that he was generally well adjusted at school and uncomplainingly participated in all the activities, even those he did not like. The handicraft lessons – seen by most as an enjoyable part of the school routine – were a burden to Kai. He invariably gave his all and could present a completed piece of work every time, but was always the last to finish. Whenever such a detested handicraft session was on the schedule, I wondered why it was not possible to take Kai's young age into consideration and to perhaps give him another, less demanding task. After all, it is a frustrating experience for children like Kai to be shown time and again that a clever little mind is only worth its salt if one's hands are no less skilful.

*

During Kai's time at primary school in Berlin, we parents had the task of satisfying his curiosity with various extracurricular activities. We attended afternoon educational events at Urania – a scientific society open to the public – and enrolled Kai at a Saturday school that offered philosophy courses for children. We did not do this to give him a head start in knowledge over the other children, but because our son demanded exactly this type of additional support due to his exuberant intellectual activity. In modern giftedness research, this constant impulse to acquire knowledge and the persistent search for truth are seen as a sign of intellectual giftedness[6], but it is also emphasised that intellectual sensitiveness can by no means be equated with intelligence, nor can it give an indication of future success at school. Rather, it is concerned with a child's endeavours to analyse everything while at the same time gaining the overall picture, developing a fascination for logic and theoretical problems, a keen faculty for observation and an independent, critical intellect, and acquiring new ideas and concepts – and not least thinking about one's own thought processes. While this intellectual hunger is not manifest in all highly intelligent people, it is a characteristic of all those with intellectual giftedness. Ever since his early childhood, our son demonstrated his distinctive curiosity by his endless stream of "why" questions, which we took seriously and always tried to answer in words appropriate to his age.

To ensure that Kai did not develop an imbalance toward mental activity, we always made sure he had sufficient physical exercise. During our time in Berlin, we took Kai and his friends ice-skating every weekend in the winter months, and in the summer we went on outings to the surrounding countryside.

Even in his early days at primary school, Kai showed a remarkable

6 Dabrowski K (1996) Multilevelness of emotional and instinctive functions. Part 1: Theory and description of levels and behaviour. Lublin, Poland: Towarzystwo Naukowe Katolickiego Uniwersytetu Lubelskiego

level of social commitment. I had already noticed during our years at the Children's Club that Kai often stood up for his friends with great enthusiasm. His distinctive sense of empathy, especially towards weak and disadvantaged children, became increasingly pronounced in his schooldays. I still clearly remember how vehemently our six-year-old first-grader protested against the decision to make a foreign girl from his class repeat a year. I could not calm him down, and the next day he resolutely strode into the headmaster's office to explain to him that his poor classmate was not responsible for her inadequate knowledge of German. Kai's commitment of course did not prove successful, but his fearless intervention met with astonishment. Some years later, when he was ten, he took a protective stance for a friend who had been threatened by her mother and stayed with the girl until the mother relented. Kai's short life was marked by many more such examples of empathy and moral courage that gave rise to a blend of amazement and respect among our circle of acquaintances.

During those first school years, we were pleasantly surprised at how well our special child was accepted in his various classes. Kai found friends at school in both Oslo and Berlin, and he was very well integrated. I never could have imagined this would all change within only a matter of months.

Our move to the country and the first major crisis

Once Kai had successfully completed his second school year, we made a decision that had far-reaching consequences. My husband was offered a job at the University of Bonn, and we moved to an outlying rural area where housing space was more affordable. Of course, I had been wondering how well our son would adjust to living in the country, but in my enthusiasm for this new phase of life awaiting us, I cast all doubts aside and instead thought back to our brief tranquil strolls through the woods of Norway, pictured in my mind's eye a cosy country school with small, quiet classes and imagined Kai in the midst of a happy throng of children on their way to school in the morning. I was convinced I had done the right thing. It was only later that I came to realise we had deprived Kai of an important basis for development with our decision to turn our backs on the city, with its wide range of intellectual stimuli.

We moved into our cottage amidst the greenery, settled in and set out to establish contact with the village community. Country life was a new experience for all of us, and I too had to reorient myself. I never would have thought it would be so difficult to establish more than mere superficial acquaintances. Kai fared no differently: he tried his hardest to make new friends, but could not manage to break into the established cliques. When he saw that all his schoolmates played football, he also wanted to join in and we registered him with the local football club; but he was only rarely part of the action, since the other children usually made him goalkeeper. Although Kai soon realised he could not develop genuine enthusiasm for the sport, he played along nevertheless, because he wanted at all costs to avoid being an outsider. We parents also did our best to help Kai make contact with the village children, for example by sending them invitations to Kai's birthday parties. But it was all to no avail – Kai remained an outsider in the eyes of the local children.

To our great disappointment, the situation developed no differently at school. Kai, now in third grade, sat alone on his bench, because the other children had already known one another for a long time and had formed couples or firmly established small groups that granted no admission to newcomers. The lessons were tormenting for Kai, since this school did not provide special didactic programmes for gifted pupils. He was bored for most of the time at school, and a further problem was that he had nobody with whom he could really talk. When I once approached his teacher, she assured me that Kai was a very dear pupil, but added that my son had not been able to establish close connections to his classmates.

We tried to compensate for Kai's lack of real challenges at school with various activities. In this process, we came to realise just how limited the offers were in our rural environment. Unlike in Berlin, there were neither educational events nor philosophy courses on offer – there was simply nothing that could have challenged Kai's lively

Kai as a fourth-grader

intellect. I was also disappointed to see that my son had now grown out of taking walks through the woods, which he had loved so much in Norway. On the other hand, we regularly visited the public baths – an activity we greatly enjoyed. At home we played Scrabble and party games together with my husband, watched selected television programmes and went on excursions at the weekends. We kept Kai occupied as best we could, but at the same time it was entirely clear to me that this would not be enough in the long term. I was at my wits' end.

My son's wishes for his forthcoming eighth birthday made his state of inner turmoil clear to me: as a sign of solidarity with his schoolmates his wish list included fan articles from his favourite football club, BVB Dortmund, including player portrait cards. But he also wished for a brother of the same age who would think along the same lines – and this is where the real Kai came to the fore. It broke my heart to see him in such a predicament, but for the first time I was unable to help him.

When a play was staged at the school and Kai's role consisted of just one single word, we knew that he was starting to withdraw himself emotionally and intellectually.

*

I by no means wish to criticise Kai's teacher for the lack of support he had been receiving. How could I? At that time, in the mid-nineties, teachers had simply not been sensitised to the needs of gifted children, and most primary schools – particularly in rural areas – were lacking a differentiated syllabus appropriate to their level of performance. Much has improved over the past twenty years: each school board now has its own mentor for gifted pupils, who can provide support and advice should problems arise at school. Teachers are given sound insights into the topic of giftedness, and an increasing number of projects are being initiated for the support of gifted pupils at primary schools. This development is based on an insight which special interest associations for giftedness have already wished to see implemented for several years and is now being taken up by the political sphere to an increasing extent: the schools should also play a role in providing support for gifted children, so that this is not merely left up to the parents in afternoon or weekend courses, as is still often the case even today. A prime example of this current rethink in policy is the Declaration of Mainz from 29th February

2016, in which 13 federal states obliged themselves to treat support for high-performing and potentially gifted children and adolescents as a key responsibility of the schools. Although I am very pleased with this development, it unfortunately came about too late for my son.

*

Dark clouds had been gathering on the horizon, but I could not yet see the approaching disaster. I only noticed that something was seriously amiss when Kai became ill in fourth grade. He started to suffer from headaches – terrible migraine attacks that we had great trouble coming to terms with. The doctor we had sought out for him could not find an organic cause for this condition and spoke of a psychosomatic disorder. Medication did not help, and darkening Kai's room likewise failed to bring about any improvement. He lay apathetically in his dark room for days on end and seemed to increasingly detach himself from us. Going to school was out of the question: even when his headaches became more tolerable during merciful interludes between migraine attacks, Kai refused to attend school. Since the connection between my son's disorder and the situation at school was all too obvious, I kept him with me at home. Kai's days of illness added up to a long absence, and during this time I was constantly at pains to come by the intellectual nourishment that was so important to my son.

On one such day that school year, when Kai had been sitting alone in his room the whole morning again, he surprised me at lunchtime by announcing that he had written a story of his own. I was pleased to hear that my son's creative drive was returning and inquisitively cast my eyes over the page. My blood froze when I read this story, only a few sentences long. I read it so often in the following weeks that I can now write it down from memory:

The skunk

Once upon a time there was a skunk that didn't stink, but smelled of Boss perfume. One day he wanted to stink like all his fellow skunks. So he hit on the idea of rolling in cowpats – no sooner said than done. But to no avail. He was so annoyed that he killed himself. He then decomposed and stank. His wish had come true, and he could now rest in peace.

Today, I can see quite clearly that this story is as simple as it is brilliant. By the age of nine, Kai had already recognised that his different view of things gave him the edge over his classmates, but this status was a burden to him and there was nothing he wanted more than to be just like all the other children. There is a certain irony to this tale, which turns the story of the ugly duckling upside-down: not that which is beautiful or special is seen as desirable, but the "ugly" or the mundane, which despite all efforts remains unattainable. But what struck me with full force on that day when Kai showed me his story was my son's death wish, which he had now expressed for the first time. I could never have imagined that my nine-year-old was struggling with such thoughts. I was plagued with terrible self-reproach: how could I have remained oblivious to Kai's desolate emotional state for so long?

Kai often spoke of suicide in the following years, and the older he became, the more concrete form his thoughts assumed. We were alarmed every time by his remarks, which took on increasingly clear contours. We of course tried to find out the exact reason for Kai's mental torment, but our son was not willing or able to divulge anything of his motives, and his repeated answer "There's no sense to it all" merely pointed to a vague weltschmerz that was difficult to identify. In his daily routine my husband was able to suppress and even forget these unsettling thoughts about Kai's emotional despair, but this was not possible for me and each of these episodes caused me terrible anguish.

This first indication that Kai was thinking of suicide, when he was in fourth grade, made me absolutely determined to seek professional help. I could not simply sit back and accept the fact that a nine-year-old child saw the solution to his problems in suicide! I took Kai to a nearby psychiatric clinic. The doctors carried out various tests with him and finally announced their diagnosis: Kai suffered from autism, and they recommend treatment in a day clinic. Nobody was willing to take up my objection that Kai's behavioural disturbances could just as well be a result of his giftedness, a condition that had been definitively confirmed. I could not and would not accept the diagnosis of autism, which to me was clearly wrong. I consulted our GP and together we decided not to begin treatment at the day clinic.

I can say with certainty today that Kai was not autistic. On the contrary: throughout his life, he was a very sociable person with a strong need for human contact. Kai was never a loner, and he had at least one or two friends even in the darkest phases of his life. On the other hand, a more recent study has shown that gifted children with a passionate interest in topics that others may find strange are often wrongly diagnosed with the Asperger syndrome, a mild form of autism.[7] I do not know whether a false assessment of Kai's giftedness played a role in this diagnosis. But our experience with the clinic showed me once more that whether I liked it or not, I would have to take care of my son myself. I decided that a secondary school would be the best solution, and so I set out in search of a grammar school that could adequately cater to Kai's needs.

*

There were nevertheless some happy moments in this overwhelmingly bleak period of Kai's life. A young cat that had befriended Kai on the street was one of these few rays of hope. We kept the cat, and it became a much-loved member of our family until Kai developed a cat hair allergy and we had to give it away. When I recall this cat today, I think of it as "gifted" because it saved a child's life. I had been told that a neighbour of ours once wanted to reverse his car onto the street. He no doubt would have run over a small child who was absent-mindedly playing behind the car in the street if the cat had not stubbornly remained sitting next to the front wheel. The man got out to shoo the cat away. It was only when he was standing next to his car that he noticed the crouching child behind it, who miraculously remained unharmed. From that time on, Kai saw the cat as a talisman and loved it all the more. When it became obvious that we would not be able to keep the animal because of his allergy, Kai was

7 Probst B (2007) When your child's second exceptionality is emotional: Looking beyond psychiatric diagnosis. 2e Twice Exceptional Newsletter, 20, 1 and 19-23

heartbroken. Unfortunately, we could not fulfil his wish for another pet, such as a dog, since we simply lacked the time.

Another ray of hope in those days was the Nintendo console with video games, for which Kai developed great enthusiasm. He was interested not so much in the games themselves, but in their inner workings. The Nintendo console that we had bought him so that he could at least have this small pleasure was often besieged by his classmates. They gladly took up Kai's invitation and spent hours on end playing shooting games while Kai sat alongside, happy to receive these rare visits and wondering to himself how the games had been developed. He not only devoured the relevant magazines, which I always had to buy for him, but also made a Nintendo magazine of his own, for which he wrote reviews of the games himself or downloaded them from the Internet. He eagerly devised several issues of this magazine on the computer under his father's supervision. When the information from the periodicals no longer met his needs, he wrote to the Nintendo headquarters in the Franconian town of Grossostheim near Aschaffenburg to request further material. Kai was overjoyed when he was given an invitation from the Nintendo company. He was received by the managing director of the European headquarters in Grossostheim, was treated to a Fanta and was invited to talk shop with the game advisers about the latest video games. As a reward for his interest he was given countless games for his console, which he then proudly presented to his classmates at home.

Kai soon came to realise that video games – especially the shooting games – were not only a fascinating pastime, but also a psychological danger for children. Since he saw it as his duty to warn of this hazard, our eleven-year-old sent a letter to a newspaper with the heading *"No violence in video games"*. His letter started with the words: *"I am a child and I am 11 years old, and I now want to awaken the interest of all parents. There are very many video games that glorify violence [...]. But first of all, I want to enlighten you as to just how brutal these games are."* This he did in lucid detail, and his letter concluded with the words: *"Do not let your children play these games, and take all such games away from them [...], and take rigorous action."* With this insight video games were now a closed book for him; he sold all his games and the console and then only used the computer – at first mainly for creative work, and later also for surfing on the Internet.

*

Kai gradually recovered from his illness and could return to school. However, the headmaster was concerned about Kai's long absence and insisted that he be tested on the fourth-grade syllabus. Together we found an outside teacher who assumed this task. The headmaster recommended that Kai take private tuition in preparation for this test, but I trusted in my son's abilities and we dismissed this suggestion. Kai did not disappoint me: in this test, he showed that he already mastered not only the material for fourth grade, but also some of the fifth-grade syllabus. So he had no difficulty in following the lessons after his illness, and at the end of fourth grade he was recommended for grammar school despite his long absence. When his last school day was approaching, Kai decided to give a farewell present to his teacher, whom he very much admired. He bought a small necklace and a ring from his pocket money and asked her to wear them in remembrance of him.

Kai's primary school years had come to an end. Attending grammar school marked the beginning of a new era, which initially let us breathe a sigh of relief and forget the "skunk" days. But in view of what then followed, the problems of his primary school years paled by comparison and we were driven to despair.

Grammar school days with highs and lows

We registered Kai, who had now turned nine, at a grammar school with an integrated class for gifted pupils that had been opened only short time beforehand in a neighbouring town. The school motto "No one may be lost" filled me with confidence, since it expressed the will to successfully accompany even gifted "problem children" through their schooling. After the experiences of Kai's skunk days, I attached special significance to this credo.

His start at the new school was indeed promising. Already after his first day there my son ran towards me with a smile all over his face: "Mama, this is a completely different school!" he declared. He particularly enjoyed the extracurricular project groups. Kai decided to join the school choir and took courses in English and chess as well as a computer course, which over the years provided him with a firm foundation in computer science. Unfortunately, this was also the time when Kai developed an aversion to sport, which – in combination with an unrestrained appetite that he developed after his skunk days – soon gave rise to concern about his weight. In the lower grades at school there had not yet been any indication of his later weight gain, however: the photos from that time showed a slim boy who differed the most strikingly from his younger self by reason of his tinted curls, now resplendent in dark maroon.

Kai rapidly made friends at his new school. In particular, at an age when girls and boys start to distance themselves from each other, he showed no signs of turning away from the opposite sex. Kai's classmate Sophia, who developed a close friendship with him in later years, looks back: *"Kai didn't join in the preadolescent disputes between girls and boys: it didn't matter to him whether his friends were boys or girls. That's why I too could go to the Nintendo parties at his place and hold the controller in my hand during the game marathon. I still remember those first encounters with Kai very well. They were fun and exciting, and I always had the feeling of being in another world."*

Also remarkable was the fearless self-confidence that Kai already showed at that age; this made a great impression on his classmates. Sophia continues her recollections of Kai: *"We were on a class excursion, and Kai dragged an amazingly heavy sport bag up the stairs of the youth hostel. 'Hey Kai, what have you got in that bag?' somebody asked. 'My ration of cola for the next few days,' he said. But he then had to hand it in, once the teachers got wind of it. As a child I was shocked that he had even dared to do that, but at the same time I found it incredibly brave."* Kosima, a friend and companion of my son in later years, also still remembers Kai's inimitable behaviour at that time: *"I remember when I was new in sixth grade at the grammar school and Kai immediately stood out from the other boys. He was always prepared to take up a courageous discussion with the teachers. That was really impressive, especially at his young age."*

Kai was also popular with the teachers in those early days, and even today some of them still smile when they think back to my argumentative, humorous and highly astute son. When I met his former English teacher recently and asked her what she most vividly remembered about her encounters with Kai, she told me something I had not known before that brought a smile to my face: when the teacher gave Kai's class a written test one day, she was surprised to see on collecting the papers that two small bags of gummy bears were attached to my son's test. In answer to her queries Kai mischievously responded: "They'll help you cope with your frustration when you correct my work!" The teacher was astonished by such directness, but also appreciated the humour of the situation. She also remembered Kai's untiring fight for justice that erupted whenever somebody from his class felt wrongly treated, for instance when he or she did not agree with a test assessment. She assured me that Kai was very popular with the children at that time and had many friends.

Driven by his keen sense of justice, Kai discovered a new field of interest towards the end of his time in junior school: law. For his forthcoming twelfth birthday he requested a copy of the German Civil Code, in which he then incessantly browsed. His preoccupation with this tome reinforced his decision to study law after finishing school. But even before this time, he acquired a comprehensive knowledge of civil law through the Civil Code and his Internet research, which he presented to his family friends in the form of "legal advice sessions".

All in all, we were satisfied with our son's development throughout his first years at grammar school. Much to my delight I only heard positive reports of Kai at the parents' evenings: I had no need to worry, I was told, as he contributed a great deal in class and performed well. But the most beautiful words of praise for my child came from the deputy headmaster, who spoke of Kai as "our sunshine" when I visited him once for a consultation. Things could basically not have been any better, I thought to myself, and could sit back and relax for the first time since Kai's enrolment in primary school. At last I could pass on to the school the responsibility that had been weighing down on my shoulders for a number of years. In our family, we now increasingly turned to the "pleasant things of life": we organised children's birthday parties, the three of us played parlour games, we watched television together and talked a great deal. I felt secure, because there was as yet no sign of the problems that would soon hit us with full force.

*

In those days, when I could breathe a sigh of relief for the first time again in a long time, I started to make new professional plans. During the years after our move into the country, I wistfully thought back time and again to the Children's Club that I had managed so successfully in Berlin, and it became increasingly clear to me that I still felt an attachment to this project. So with my new plans I wanted to continue the concept of the Children's Club, but this time I had something bigger on my mind: I planned to establish a support facility for gifted children of preschool and school age, and consciously chose a location in the country not far from my home. Given my own painful experience, it was important to me to promote the extension of educational facilities for gifted children in a rural environment.

The "Children's College" opened in 2000. In several stages, I expanded the promotional institution and made it what it is today: a Saturday school where in each half-year 500 to 900 pupils aged three to sixteen can find an intellectual and emotional home. The Children's College now offers around 80 courses that the children and adolescents can take in accordance with their inclinations. The demand was high from the outset, and current enrolment figures show that the need for extracurricular promotional offers for gifted children is no less acute today.

We give a lot of thought to the choice of our teachers, who especially in the courses for older children are intellectually on a par with the pupils. I believe that for gifted young people, dialogue with committed teachers is at least as important as the purely intellectual challenge. In view of Kai's schooling odyssey, I experienced for myself just how much of a strain it can often be for a teacher-pupil relationship when the teacher cannot put himself or herself in the position of a gifted pupil. This invariably gives rise to tension, so that the teacher meets with less acceptance and the pupil's motivation to become actively involved in the classes is seriously impaired.

The Children's College has now become my purpose in life. It fills me with joy and satisfaction when I can actively support gifted children and their often desperate parents. And it is not without a certain pride that I can see our work now bearing fruit to an increasing extent above and beyond the personal level: the facility is highly esteemed even outside Germany and is financially supported by the state of Rhineland-Palatinate. I regard the recognition of our work by the political sphere as a milestone, since it shows that giftedness is seen as a phenomenon relevant to society and that the calls for commitment towards these children and adolescents do not go unheard.

*

Kai's problems started in eighth grade, shortly after he had embarked on the intermediate level at his grammar school. There had been a change of teachers, with a new intermediate head, and the climate in the classrooms had suddenly become harsher. In the lessons, reprimands and punishment were increasingly used as a means of discipline; this posed a challenge to Kai's libertarian spirit and moved him to protest whenever he sensed injustice. An atmosphere gradually evolved in which my son no longer felt accepted and to which he was increasingly opposed. Moreover, the highly popular project work, a special support measure, was discontinued and only conventional classes were offered.

At the same time, Kai started to change physically. His insatiable appetite and lack of exercise now started to tell on him, and his formerly slim figure became more corpulent. At an age when no other teenager would have come up with the idea, he started to wear black suits – preferably of the Boss brand. He discarded his school satchel in favour of an aluminium briefcase. Most of Kai's classmates accepted his new look, because they understood – much earlier than many an adult – that the suits and aluminium briefcase were part of Kai's new image. His classmate and later close friend Sophia remembers how my son's appearance was simply taken for granted at that time:

"'Who's that young man with the briefcase?' my father asked.

"'That's Kai; he always goes around like that!' I answered.

"The sense of normality that this frequent reply suggested in my early years at grammar school did not arise from my self-confident nature or my carefree childlike attitude. It was due to this boy himself, who – usually clothed all in black – carried his briefcase through the schoolyard just like other children carry their satchels.

"It was just the entirely natural way he did it. So for me, there was nothing to discuss, ridicule or put into question.

"That's Kai; he always goes around like that."

It was a different matter with his teachers. Some were not overly concerned about Kai's new look, but his overall acceptance at the school started to suffer. "You with your silly briefcase" was just one of the comments he had to hear from the teachers. Kai's dwindling acceptance among the teaching staff was also no doubt due to the onset of puberty. He had exhausted his "child's bonus". Together with his changed appearance, his argumentative character – which had been manifest from the outset – was now increasingly seen as a provocation and was treated accordingly; this further reinforced Kai's desire to withdraw himself.

I began to understand that an era had just come to an end for my son: the era of conformity. What now painfully made its way to the surface was the real, genuine Kai, having risen like Phoenix from the ashes. The floodgates were opened, and all I could now do was to wait and see what havoc this torrent would wreak.

*

It was at this time that I first noticed something about Kai which could be described as suffering at the hands of the world – the world of people. This weltschmerz firmly took hold of him over the following years and became an intricate part of his nature. I saw this development in close connection with his keen interest in global events: Kai became more and more of a walking dictionary – he knew at least something about everything, and he soaked up all available information like a sponge and then reproduced it. However, what he gleaned from news reports, magazines, television programmes and the Internet was anything but a "beautiful" world: hunger and misery in Africa, inhuman oppression in North Korea, hatred and violence in the Middle East, fanatical Islamists who randomly murdered innocent people the world over, human traffickers, child abusers and child pornography rings, even in the so-called first world – in brief: many millions of innocent people who suffered at the hands of others.

Anyone with a sense of empathy will find all the evils of this world terrible, but despite all consternation it is unusual to be incessantly preoccupied with how bad and unjust the world is. One is gladly sidetracked by trifling everyday matters – what to wear or buy, whether to go to the pub or sit in front of the television set in the evening – and can make everyday decisions and forget for a moment the suffering of the world. I am convinced that the situation was different with Kai: he too of course thought about what he should put on or buy, or whether he should watch television in the evening, but his awareness of the condition of the world constantly accompanied him. In everything he did, the plight of this world was always present in his thoughts. And for him, this meant that he also permanently thought about the meaning of the world and the meaning of life – and above all the meaninglessness of life. While I merely found all this terrible and could simply get back to my routine, Kai genuinely suffered from it.

Just like his extremely pronounced sense of justice, I could only understand Kai's excessive weltschmerz and put it into context several years later, when I studied Dabrowski's personality theory. According to Dabrowski, these character traits are an indication of a highly developed emotional sensitivity and are therefore a variety of intellectual giftedness. Extreme emotional sensitivity is accompanied on the one hand by complex, passionate feelings, a strong, differentiated experience of emotions and a pronounced empathic capacity, but also by shyness, excitability, psychosomatic disorders, intense memories of feelings, fears, thoughts of death, depression and at times even contemplation of suicide. Remarks frequently made by those affected include: "I feel different all the time", "I want to be normal", "I don't belong" or "I don't know what I'm doing here". Not only one's own feelings, however, but also the emotions, fears and tensions of others, can be experienced as overwhelming. High emotional sensitivity thus generates an empathy that can be both very useful and extremely taxing.[8]

According to Dabrowski's theory, which I have already briefly mentioned in connection with Kai's sensitivity to noise, an individual's potential for development is at its peak when all forms of sensational capacity – psychomotoric, sensory, intellectual, imaginative and emotional – are strongly present. But a high level of emotional capacity is the most influential factor, and it is only the combination

8 Braham A, Schneider-Maessen S (2010) Dabrowskis Bezug zur Praxis: Das Konzept des hohen Empfindungsvermögens – ein erweiterter Blick auf Hochbegabung. Journal für Hochbegabung, 2, 42-47

of high emotional, intellectual and imaginative capacity that provides the basis for ongoing inner development. When I think of Kai's innate character today, I realise that he fully met all the requirements for personal development.

*

During that school year, in which things were already going anything but smoothly for Kai, we met with a further disappointment – this time in connection with his forthcoming confirmation. The lessons for confirmation candidates were on the schedule for eighth grade, and since we already suspected Kai would decline to participate in the conventional confirmation lessons, we set out in search of a suitable alternative.

We had no doubt that Kai should be confirmed. Even as a small child, he had already been fascinated by the major aspects of the Christian faith – above all the suffering, death and resurrection of Jesus Christ – but his naive childlike interest had rapidly given way to a critical questioning of theology and of the faith itself. His preoccupation with religious matters, and now also to an increasing extent with the world religions in general, was however still important to him, and we wanted to encourage him in this. Our idea was to have a parish priest and professor of theology well known to us carry out the preparations for Kai's confirmation. This professor was an expert in world religions, and he would have been able to provide Kai with a good academic grounding and discuss with him theological matters and – most importantly – the meaning of life.

However, the vicar responsible for the confirmation lessons insisted that Kai take a look at the classes. Kai enquired as to what was on the curriculum. At the first meeting the candidates were asked to draw up "wanted" posters, and the second consisted of a bicycle tour. Kai declined to participate: as an eighth-grader he felt he had long since outgrown the former, and the latter did not interest him. As we had already suspected, he then refused to attend the confirmation lessons at all. We were not given permission to involve the professor of theology, and so Kai was not confirmed. Shortly afterwards he drew the consequences from this hapless interlude and insisted on officially leaving the church.

To this day, I cannot understand why the church did not want to take up our suggestion. We would have gladly borne the costs of the lessons ourselves; and in any case, the confirmation itself should have been the decisive factor, not the preparations for it. The church was perhaps displeased that we had requested special treatment for our son, but this was typical of Kai: we often had to go to great lengths with him to attain something that was completely normal and natural for others – such as a school leaving qualification, or now his confirmation. I would have hoped for more support from the church on our stony path, especially since I had been an active member of the church for many years. I still feel this as a bitter disappointment today.

The second fall

A development that had already set in during eighth grade finally came to a head in Kai's ninth school year: he again refused to attend school. It was clear to me that he did this not to be rebellious, but because he simply could not do any differently. As a highly sensitive person, he was completely overwhelmed by his intense emotions, and I felt deeply sorry for him in his helplessness. At first, I had hoped this would be a mere passing phase, but the weeks and months passed by and Kai was still unable to return to school. Not only was he lacking the necessary strength; he was plagued once more by intense migraine attacks, which he now treated himself – unlike in primary school – with a cocktail of painkillers and caffeine. But not even this could cure his inability to attend school, so that Kai finally left his grammar school at the age of fourteen.

This came as a shock to me. I failed to understand why my highly intelligent son, who had no end of opportunities open to him, had now quite obviously failed at school. He did not even have a lower school certificate! I resolved to leave no stone unturned in helping Kai earn his leaving qualification. But first of all, it was important to me to have Kai's IQ tested once more – even if only to determine the cause of our plight. Moreover, Kai was now at an age when the result of an IQ test could be seen as relatively reliable.

And so we had Kai tested a second time. As I had already suspected, the outcome showed that he was in fact highly gifted. Kai was thus intellectually on a par with the likes of Stephen Hawking, Bill Gates, Hillary Clinton and Albert Einstein, or the former chess world champion Garry Kasparov, who was attested an extremely high level of intelligence in a renowned IQ test.

Although a high IQ is generally equated with giftedness, current talent research has shown that this is not merely the result of an unusually high level of intelligence. A high IQ is a prerequisite, but not the only necessary factor for giftedness: decisive is an individual's personal development, which is also substantially dependent on one's sensitivity and will for growth.[9,10] According to this interpretation, an intelligence test quantifies only the talent itself, but does not predict its further development.

Kai was already aware at a young age that intelligence alone can give no indication of a person's inner nature. Even in his early grammar school days, he could already distinguish between eccentrics and "normal" gifted pupils – and numbered himself among the latter. An open-minded, generous person, he not only always stood up for his friends as a matter of course, but it came just as naturally to him to join in and have fun, and in later years to be part of the action at parties.

---

9 Dabrowski K (1996) Multilevelness of emotional and instinctive functions. Part 1: Theory and description of levels and behaviour. Lublin, Poland: Towarzystwo Naukowe Katolickiego Uniwersytetu Lubelskiego

10 Tillier W (2002) A brief overview of the relevance of Dabrowski's theory of the gifted, In AGATE, 15(2), pp. 4–12

*

After Kai had left school in ninth grade and then practically only stayed at home for months on end, he became lonely. He still had neither friends in our neighbourhood nor any other good contacts who could have supported him in his crisis. It was only later that he made friends with a boy and his family from own town. Their relationship became so close that they once even took him with them on holiday. During the time of crisis, however, when Kai no longer went to school, his lack of contacts in our neighbourhood forced him into a social isolation that he by no means wanted and which he could not bear for long.

He started going to the youth centre of our neighbouring community in the evenings. I welcomed this development at first, because he was obviously seeking company. But I then soon noticed that the contacts he established there were by no means helpful to him. Adolescents that I had never seen before and who did not inspire much confidence in me now started coming and going in our house at will. Kai made acquaintance with alcohol under their influence, but his first experiences with it were apparently so negative that he abstained from drinking after an initial phase of "being one of the boys". He remained in contact with this group nevertheless. I know today – for example from conversations with friends of my son's in whom he later confided – that Kai neither shared nor approved of the fundamental attitudes of his companions and even exposed them as foolish. But he still stayed with them. Kai only pulled the plug when one of his new "friends" got into trouble with the police and he was summoned as a witness. He then stopped visiting the youth centre on his own initiative. This episode in Kai's life gave me cause for concern at the time; but in hindsight, I see it today as what it no doubt was: the desperate attempt of an emotionally homeless boy to find security and recognition in a group of peers.

*

During Kai's second deep crisis I once more felt the helplessness that our problems imposed not only on society, but also on the field of science. For my own part, dealing with Kai's emotional crises was like running the gauntlet: my sole objective was now to summon up all available resources to keep my son from abandoning all hope. How relieved I would have been to be able to pass on this responsibility or at least to get some well-founded help! But my wish did not come true, even when I decided to take Kai to the clinic once more, despite our previous negative experience with psychiatric diagnoses. A doctor examined Kai and this time identified ADS, the attention deficit syndrome; she recommended that he be treated with the psychotropic drug Ritalin. To me this was clearly another false assessment of the situation: I knew Kai as no other person did, and I sensed that his refusal to attend school was solely due to his exceptional talents and abilities, which merely proved a hindrance in the daily routine of a conventional school. What I had been hoping for on the part of medical science was "instructions" for dealing with his difficulties – but these apparently did not exist.

Even today, psychologists and psychiatrists are still groping in the dark in their assessment of children like Kai and therefore tend to unjustifiably pathologise such situations. Piechowski writes on this topic: "*It is a common mistake to take something exceptional as being abnormal. (...) Unfortunately so many years later the tendency to pathologize and try to correct the expressions of overexcitability with medication or discipline, is still very much with us. It plagues many gifted children attending public schools. For instance, one of the most common misjudgements is to label as hyperactive a child full of energy and vitality. A truly hyperactive AD/HD child cannot control it, but an energetic child can and becomes focused when engaged in something interesting.*"[11] This statement, which I came across many years after Kai left school, confirms in retrospect that I was right in mistrusting the clinic's ADS diagnosis. It had always been quite clear to me that Kai's preparedness to actively participate in classes depended only on the syllabus offered.

Nor I do think that Kai suffered from a classic depression. He did have a great need for sleep at the times that he suffered from migraine, but he was constantly active and enjoyed the company of others. In the many conversations I had with him at that time, he also showed me quite clearly that he knew about depression and did not think it relevant to his situation. We still had a good relationship and could talk about many things, but I could not get to the bottom of this one question of what exactly had triggered his inner crisis. Whenever he mentioned to us his alarming thoughts of suicide, he would simply say that he saw no sense in it all. And I am convinced that this oppressive feeling of senselessness was rooted in Kai's mind and not in his soul.

---

11 Piechowski MM (2010) Ein Vogel, der zur Sonne emporsteigen kann: Erhöhte Sensitivität der Begabten. Journal für Begabtenförderung. 2:7-21

*

Unfortunately, an emotional crisis can often give rise to depression in gifted children even at a young age. Each and every child who suffers this fate is one child too many: depression is a serious personality disorder from which all children should be spared. In many cases it is triggered by the negative self-image these children develop as a result of marginalisation at school and in other established groups, where they stand out as being different, are often dismissed as being "difficult" and are ultimately rejected.

Throughout my long years of professional practice, I myself have not generally found it difficult to deal with gifted children and adolescents. Even among the gifted "problem children" so dreaded by schools, conflicts at the Children's College are few and far between. On the basis of my experience I can say that two factors are decisive for peaceful coexistence and a productive learning atmosphere: acceptance and respect. I can confirm that gifted young people who feel accepted and are treated with the same respect as adults develop autonomously and basically have no need to have their behaviour corrected with pedagogical measures. The ideal situation is when the pupils and teachers are equally gifted, since the teachers then encounter their smart pupils at eye level and cannot be demoralised even by the more rebellious ones among them. It is not helpful to put the more difficult pupils under pressure and to insist on fixed rules for studying and classwork. This did not work with Kai, and it generally fails to work with gifted children and adolescents with a nonconformist, libertarian disposition.

The principles of acceptance and respect can apparently be more easily implemented in a Saturday school, which is not concerned with leaving qualifications, than in a conventional school – even though the personality of the teacher, and the way in which he or she conveys the material and motivates the children, can no doubt play an important role independently of the type of school. It is therefore all the more pleasing that politicians are now providing more support for gifted children and adolescents and that more and more special schools for gifted pupils are being opened; on the other hand, it gives me cause for concern that many of these schools set out to make a name for themselves as high-performance institutes that are highly suitable for ambitious children, but where less conformist youngsters still fall by the wayside. It is apparently not sufficient for these "problem cases" to be given schooling together with their intellectual peers but still in accordance with conventional teaching methods. This insight is now gaining more and more acceptance at schools. The grammar school with an integrative class for gifted pupils, for example, which Kai attended up until ninth grade, has now discarded its original motto "No one may be lost". The new motto is "We are the givers of opportunity" – which better reflects the possibilities of pedagogical support for gifted pupils.

*

In our darkest days, when it became clear that Kai would not be returning to his grammar school, I gave a great deal of thought as to how I could free my son from his deep crisis. I was absolutely determined to fight for my son and his future with all the means at my disposal. Once I had confided my thoughts to Kai's physician, we together decided that I would offer my son a language and culture tour. Since Kai had been interested in foreign languages, geography and politics from an early age, I was optimistic that he would take up my suggestion. We decided on Malta, and I made him the – quite expensive – offer of a language tour. The fact that we would sacrifice our annual holidays for this undertaking was not important to me at the time. All that mattered was that I had finally managed to dispel the gloom from Kai's thoughts. To my great relief Kai consented, and the journey was a great success. He really flourished in the mild Mediterranean climate of the island with its blue sky, sea and wind. He became acquainted with the land and its people and developed a good relationship with his host family. These friendly Maltese took Kai warm-heartedly under their wing, but also granted him many liberties, so that he by no means felt restricted or too closely monitored. Of course, I had some doubts the whole time as to whether all would be well with my fourteen-year-old so far away, but my concerns were unfounded. Kai came back rested and full of enthusiasm. Most importantly, he now appeared so stable that we could give serious consideration to the matter of school once more. I felt immense relief.

*

It seems like a miracle to me today that we had managed to catch Kai in his second fall. This was an unbelievably nerve-racking time, in which I had to mobilise all my forces. So I was all the more pleased that Kai appreciated my commitment to him: at that time, I received an "Oscar" for the world's best mother – a gesture that went very much to my heart.

Back to school

After his time in Malta, I managed to convince Kai to return to school the following autumn. But going back to his old grammar school was out of the question. At a conventional school he would also have had to repeat ninth grade, which he refused out of hand. After careful consideration I decided to enrol my son at a private educational institute in nearby Bonn, in preparation for the special examination for children who do not attend a regular school. Passing this examination would entitle him to advance to the senior level at grammar school.

Kai felt relatively at ease at his new school. This was essentially due to two teachers whom he very much admired, and the fact that he could study more or less autonomously. Although he had missed almost all of ninth grade, he had no difficulties with the syllabus: he demonstrated once more what intellectual achievements he was capable of as long as he was sufficiently motivated. It was a great relief for me to see my son with something to aim for once again.

In my preparations for this book I asked Bernd Mischke, one of Kai's favourite teachers from the institute in Bonn with whom I am still in contact today, to relate his memories of my son. He told me of

Kai's brilliance, which came to light whenever he was genuinely interested in something. On the other hand, he also remembered Kai's listlessness and lack of participation in topics that did not hold him captivated, the calculated optimism that he occasionally demonstrated, and his strategic, minimalistic approach to mastering the subject matter.

He vividly recalled my son's distinctive appearance, with his black suits. He remembered the other pupils' respect for Kai and the fascination they showed for his well-founded contributions to class discussions. He was never bullied. The teacher also recalled a further detail: Kai was open-minded and very tolerant of other opinions, but only when they were well considered and were not based on false premises. It was important to him to be able to enter into discussion with people. But he gave short shrift to unfounded, superficially aired views that put paid to meaningful discussion.

As the school year was drawing to a close, we applied for special permission from the Ministry of Education so that Kai could sit for the special examination for non-school attenders: only candidates at least sixteen years old were normally admitted to this external examination, and Kai was only fifteen at the time. Despite his problematical past experience, Kai had no trouble passing the examination and was allowed to attend senior grammar school.

*

One of the examiners for this test was Andreas Breitenstein, now principal of the secondary modern school of the Christian youth organisation CJD in Königswinter. Breitenstein knew Kai from earlier times because he had taught him at his lower-level grammar school. In a letter to me, he remembered Kai's distinctive appearance at this school and his brilliance in the external examination:

"When Kai was in seventh grade at our school, I taught him art in the 1998/1999 school year. He had his own way of expressing himself in art, but he was a good pupil. After that year I occasionally saw him in the schoolyard, and we exchanged a few words every time. He always wore a black suit and carried a briefcase to fit this image. I liked him. After a while I no longer saw him, because he had left the school.

"At that time, I was assessing the external examination for the regional administration in Cologne. All pupils that were taught at a supplementary school and wanted to attain a recognised school leaving qualification had to sit for this examination, which was always held in the autumn and summer.

"Together with a colleague, I was responsible for geography. In my preparations for one of these external examinations, I immediately noticed the name Kai Thieroff on the list of candidates. He was in the middle of our group of students, which made both of us examiners happy to be teachers. The tests in the morning had been fairly dreary until Kai entered the room. I had already told my colleagues that I knew Kai and that he was very intelligent. We recognised each other at once; after a brief greeting we started the examination. Kai had prepared three topics, one of which we chose for the test. His delivery was so perfect that we did not need to ask him any more questions. On the contrary, we had to curb his torrent of words, otherwise he would have exceeded the time allotted to him.

"At the examiners' conference, my colleague and I then heard just how well Kai had performed in all of his tests. I heard no more of him after that.

"My colleague and I often talked about Kai and his examination, because we didn't experience anything like that again for years to come."

*

Now that Kai had passed his external examination, he could have continued his education at any regular grammar school. However, he decided to enrol for the grammar school section of a vocational college that included economics, business administration and law on its syllabus and was thus ideally matched to his interest in legal matters. I was not entirely in favour of Kai's choice of school. I had suggested that he now prepare for the external school leaving certificate through the educational institute in Bonn. He then could have worked at his own pace and also skipped one of the three long school years if necessary. But Kai stuck with his decision and I gave up trying to persuade him otherwise, because I absolutely wanted to avoid jeopardising the balance in his life that he had only found with great difficulty.

In addition to the range of subjects offered, there was another aspect that played an important role for Kai in his choice of school. The vocational college he had chosen was in Cologne, and since commuting every day was out of the question, we had to look for accommodation for him in the city. What this all entailed – life in a big city, fresh impulses, liberty, independence – was exactly what Kai wanted. We rented a centrally situated small flat for him in Genter Strasse, which he moved into with pleasure. I did not want to experiment with other forms of accommodation such as boarding school, a hostel or subtenancy, since it was clear to me that my son would no longer conform to such regulated living conditions. I therefore had to release Kai into a life of independence at the age of only fifteen, and with a heavy heart I had to get used to the idea of only having him close to me at the weekends and during school holidays.

Despite his young age, Kai was not at all overwhelmed by the liberty and independence he had suddenly attained. He managed his own household except for his laundry, which I washed for him at the weekends. He did his own shopping, learnt to cook and when he visited us at home he often impressed us with his creative, highly imaginative culinary skills.

At first, I feared that this spatial separation would cause Kai to drift away from us parents, but in fact the opposite was the case: our relationship remained stable and close; and even though we now only heard what our son was prepared to reveal to us about his life, we did not have the impression of being excluded. Kai was still communicative towards us, and our frequent long telephone conversations gave me consolation despite his absence. At weekends, we parents often visited him in his "sardine tin" – as Kai called his small, cramped flat – and were given some insights into his new life.

Kai discovered his urge to travel at that time and began to visit friends the world over whenever the opportunity arose. He also took driving lessons and underwent his test during his time in Cologne. After Kai had earned his driving licence toward the end of his stay there, shortly after his eighteenth birthday, my husband gave him our old Fiat Punto. Kai adopted a sporting style of driving and thoroughly enjoyed his newly attained mobility.

As Kai gradually regained his self-confidence and joie de vivre, the colour black also disappeared from his life. His black towels were now joined by red ones, and he no longer wore only black suits. On one of our visits to Cologne we were surprised to see a large colourful picture hanging on the wall. It was unmistakable: Kai's black phase had started to erode. I could breathe a sigh of relief and turn my attention once more to my Children's College with renewed vigour.

*

When I think back to Kai's time in Cologne, I notice how alarmingly few details I can now recall. Hazy fragments of memory flash through my mind – pieces of a mosaic that has long since shattered. I can see the three of us sitting at the table in Kai's "sardine tin", my husband – as so often – with a lighted cigarette in his hand. A flake of ash falls onto the table, and with a verve that he would never have displayed in our living room, Kai jumps up to get a cloth and remove the offending particle. In another shred of memory, our son proudly leads us to the newly opened branch of a café chain, shows us the variety of coffees on offer, advises us in our choice and finally enthuses over the shot of vanilla syrup with which he had his coffee refined. Then comes a city shopping spree that takes us into a perfumery: Kai is advised by a young shop assistant who gazes at him adoringly with big eyes and puts a whole handful of perfume samples into his shopping bag as we leave. And then I remember a CD from that time, a present to my husband entitled "Father's Hits", with music that Kai had selected himself from the Internet. And there is the story that Kai proudly told us about his Syrian acquaintances who had invited him to a dinner as their only German guest. I also remember one time when I tried in vain to ring Kai. Alarmed, I sent my husband to Cologne to see after him. He was then received in the "sardine tin" by a morose Kai, who simply did not feel like answering the telephone and could not understand all the fuss. He promised to improve and kept to the rules from that time onwards.

*

During Kai's time in Cologne, there was no sign of the loneliness that had often plagued his previous life. He made friends with a few boys from the school, but his friendship with a clique of girls – six smart, friendly young women, some of whom he had still known from his grammar school days – was particularly important to him. Kai and "his girls" were inseparable. It was only after Kai's death that I came to realise just how close the bonds of this friendship were when the girls told me of their experiences. I asked them to write down their memories of Kai for me. From these conversations and notes I learnt that for these young ladies, Kai was not only a light-hearted companion always prepared to join in the fun, but also a profoundly thinking discussion partner and an emotional support in difficult times.

"Kai was an exceptional person" – writes Kosima, one of the girls from the clique – *"with a mind of his own and humour, strong conviction of his values and an incredibly big heart for those who meant something to him. He did anything but simply follow the crowd, and that's exactly why I liked him so much.*

"We girls," she continues, *"had a wonderfully positive time with Kai. He was always prepared to undertake something on a whim,*

and in this way we had some hilarious evenings, along with some spontaneous car trips to Munich. Kai had the gift of enthusing me and cheering me up when I didn't feel good. He then always said, 'Let's go – we'll go to this place and that, and we'll really experience something!' I greatly treasure these memories today, and at difficult times I try to follow exactly this maxim – not to put my head in the sand, but to busy myself with new, enjoyable topics and activities.

"As well as having a unique sense of humour, Kai was of course incomparably intelligent and quick-witted. We could talk about serious, profound topics for hours on end – for example in discussions of faith and our values. Kai was an unbelievably liberal person, and

Kai with his good friend Kosima during his time in England

this connected us very closely. (...) I think his love of Cologne and the fact that he left home so early also reflected his desire for cosmopolitan flair and tolerance. You couldn't put Kai into any pigeonhole, and that made him unique. He did his own thing, laughed out loud whenever he felt like it, and so he was like no one else. I miss Kai very much, and I'll never forget the time I spent with him."

Sophia, also one of "Kai's girls" and a friend of my son from his time at grammar school, writes of the early days of their friendship: *"Kai left our school. I don't remember which class this was in. We kept in touch; Kai always made sure of that. Friends were important to Kai – each and every one of us".* She continues about their time in Cologne: *"Kai lived in his own flat in Cologne, at the age of fifteen. I was amazed, but also impressed by the offhand way he told me this and invited me to visit him in his 'sardine tin', as Kai called it."*

She mentions an episode from their time in the senior level at grammar school in Cologne that shows just how much Kai meant to the girls' clique in those years: *"Kosima, Tini, Sonja, Nuria, Caro and I – at senior level, we were an inseparable group of girls. Kai was often in on the action when we undertook something or decided to paint the town red. There are many funny stories from that time. (...) But there was one night I'll never forget, because our cheerful atmosphere suddenly turned serious. Like many weekends beforehand, Kosima and I travelled by train to Cologne, equipped with a bottle of champagne. We were already quite tipsy by the time we went to a nightclub in the centre of town. After half an hour Kosima, for some still inexplicable reason, suddenly collapsed. Once I had finally managed to drag her out of the club and put her on a park bench, I started to panic; the situation was too much for me: I was old enough to go to a nightclub in Cologne, but apparently too young and inexperienced to manage this situation. I rang Kai and told him of our plight. He was with us not even ten minutes later. He practically carried Kosima almost all the way to his flat, while calming me down at the same time. Once he had bundled my friend into his bed, Kai and I talked for a couple of hours until Kosima came to her senses again. To help her recover, Kai bought a huge portion of chips in the middle of the night. I'll never forget that evening. Kai did everything for his friends; he was one of the most helpful and self-sacrificing people I've ever known."*

She was also impressed by his profound knowledge of many subjects: *"Kai told me a lot of things I'd never heard before. To me, his general knowledge was simply out of this world."* Kai told her for

Kai with "his girls": Kosima (centre), Sonja (right) and Nuria (left) in Kai's flat, the "sardine tin"

example about the threat many people faced of losing their land as a result of the rise in sea level due to global warming, at a time when hardly anyone was talking about it – let alone anyone so young. *"Only Kai could know something like that and tell other people about it in such an enthusiastic and inspiring way,"* says Sophia.

In another episode she describes Kai as a friend with whom one could go through thick and thin: *"Kai and I had arranged to meet one afternoon in the Chocolate Museum in Cologne. He picked me up in his black Fiat Punto. (...) For me, he even did his best to drive somewhat more sedately. When you were out with Kai, you had to be prepared for anything. He often suddenly did something really mad. Even though I sometimes found this difficult, I loved his*

In the Chocolate Museum in Cologne. Kai's genuflection before the cocoa god aroused laughter among the visitors.

unconventional nature. Our visit to the Chocolate Museum was no exception. We had uneventfully gone through some of the exhibition rooms – Kai really was interested in all the notes and information and seemed to take it all in – when we came across a shoulder-high pile of cocoa beans. An information panel that Kai read out loud told of the customs of the Aztecs involving the cocoa plant. They worshipped a certain god who was supposed to have given them this sacred plant as a present. Two seconds later, Kai fell on the knees in front of the pile of beans and worshipped the cocoa god at the top of his voice. This of course brought a smile to the faces of many visitors in the museum. I myself had to burst out laughing and even managed to capture this moment with the camera of my mobile phone. (...) This outing to the Chocolate Museum was one of the most precious and funniest undertakings that Kai and I experienced together.

"I miss Kai, my friend."

*

After Kai's death the girls gave me a commemorative album with photos from their time together with him. The photos were taken during their time in Cologne and in the following years, since they maintained their contact when Kai was already living in England. Whenever I browse through this album, I see images of friendships and an exuberant zest for life that make everything that happened afterwards seem simply unreal. These are comical, playful pictures – Kai pulling faces, with his eyes concealed behind mirrored sunglasses, cheek to cheek with a pretty girl or flanked by smiling friends, striking silly poses against various backgrounds or pretending to be drunk at the end of an evening of revelry. I look at the somewhat portly but handsome boy with his dark, combed-back curls and a touch of stubble on his chin; I see his sparkling eyes and predominantly bright clothes, and I am certain – and pleased – that he experienced many moments of happiness together with his friends.

*

The commitment that Kai had already shown for the weak and disadvantaged in his surroundings at a very early age continued undiminished at the threshold to adulthood. I know that during his years in Cologne, for example, Kai showed great dedication towards a girl in his class who suffered from depression, and he also looked after

Kai and Philipp, friends during the Cologne days

a boy with epilepsy. His dedication was often rewarded – at the vocational college in Cologne, for instance, where he was elected class representative; but he also suffered the occasional disappointment: when he was sixteen he lent all his money, 600 euros, to a friend – the only one he had in our neighbourhood – who was in a dire situation. He waited in vain for her to pay him back: his money was never returned.

Even in the face of the occasional setback, however, Kai remained firm in his conviction that especially for him as a gifted person, social commitment is a mission. He explained this in a video interview from that time: *"Intelligence is of course of benefit for social actions, but it isn't really necessary. On the other hand, it's certainly easier for an intelligent person to recognise social problems and come up with solutions, for example through creativity. What are my own social actions? I'm very active as a class representative, and if I see that people in my surroundings have problems, I try to solve them and stand up for my fellow humans. It's very important [as a gifted person] not to walk around in arrogance or ignorance with an air of conceit just because you're at an advantage over your fellow human beings – in whatever way."*

*

The only drop of bitterness in Kai's self-determined life during his time in Cologne was at school. Not only did he have little contact to his classmates; as I had already feared, the curriculum at the vocational college also failed to meet his expectations. Kai had imagined that the major topics of European economics and law would be treated from the outset, but what was in fact offered reminded him of his schooldays: although many of the subjects he took basically met with his interest, the syllabus drove him to despair once more. Most of the content failed to captivate him, and he could not identify with the learning objectives. He showed no interest in learning vocabulary in the foreign language classes, but was very enthusiastic when political or economic topics were occasionally dealt with in regional studies. In the other subjects too, Kai always needed "input" to actively participate at all. A highlight for him was a vacation traineeship that he undertook at a major firm of solicitors in Koblenz. Even though he came to realise there that right cannot be equated with justice, he was enthusiastic about the work processes he was already involved in as a trainee, and what he saw and experienced there reinforced his eagerness to study law.

Kai successfully completed twelfth grade at the vocational college and received his intermediate diploma. But in thirteenth grade, his degree year, he failed shortly before reaching his objective. My son, who had only ever learnt what was absolutely necessary for school, had miscalculated: he was still lacking some points for admittance to the university entrance certificate examination. The teachers deliberated over his case, but then advised him to repeat the year. Kai declined and left the school in February 2005 without attaining university entrance qualification.

*

This was the end of Kai's schooling. I do not know how upsetting, how oppressive or how difficult he found this experience himself. In any case, these were years marked by highs and lows that demanded a great deal of him: throughout his school career Kai had to fight for, and at times against, himself. He could not communicate to his classmates much of what was preoccupying him, and he felt either inadequately understood or unjustly treated by most of his teachers. He experienced time and again that his special talents were of no benefit to him at school – on the contrary, they were more of a hindrance. *"According to my experience,"* Kai said in an interview towards the end of his schooldays, *"individual talents are not supported at school, neither at primary nor at secondary level. I myself attended four primary schools, during which time I found that my talents were either ignored or attempts were made to put them into a certain pigeonhole."* In particular, he also found that the school system did not leave enough room for creativity: *"At my upper level at school, creativity isn't needed, promoted or required at all. If you try a different approach to things or put anything into question, it will all work against you. They obviously want to promote mindless regurgitation of facts."*

Kai's school days were now over, and he was on the threshold of a new phase of life. But none of us knew what form this would take without a school leaving certificate. I would never have thought Kai would be able to undergo a regular university education under these conditions. But he managed even this.

Student days in England

With his school report and a letter of motivation, Kai applied to several universities in the United Kingdom later that same year to study law. In his letter, he stated that he had decided on that country because of its superior university infrastructure, the shorter duration of study and the additional bonus of perfecting his English, but also because he felt inspired by this new challenge.

Unlike in Germany, in English-speaking countries the decision to accept or reject an applicant lies entirely with the university, whereby the candidate's personality plays a decisive role. Universities are prepared to accept applicants with qualifications other than the school leaving certificate if they are convinced they meet the requirements for the subjects chosen. And this was exactly Kai's speculation: he hoped to make up for his lack of a certificate with a convincing letter of motivation and the excellent reference from the law firm in Koblenz where he had spent his traineeship. This strategy proved successful: the University of Central Lancashire in England offered Kai a place to study, which he enthusiastically accepted. Kai effortlessly passed the language test stipulated for foreign applicants with top marks – in stark contrast to the assessment "sufficient" noted in his school report for his knowledge of English.

I had mixed feelings towards my son's forthcoming move to England. As a mother, I was of course reluctant in my heart to see Kai leaving for a foreign country at the age of eighteen – but my joy that he had managed to realise his childhood dream of studying law, despite all the difficulties and setbacks, far outweighed the pain of parting.

Kai organised his move to England himself. In Preston, his university town, he rented a small flat on an estate where some other students were also living, and he began his studies in September 2005. He started with a combination of legal and political studies, but later concentrated on the legal component. Kai's studies included English civil and criminal law, British constitutional law and European law. Specialisation was possible at an early stage, and Kai orientated himself towards European and economic law. His final examinations, which would earn him the academic degree LL.B., Bachelor of Laws, were planned for June 2008.

To this day, it still seems unreal to me that this never came about: from the moment Kai bade farewell to his schooldays and could start with his long-awaited study of law, absolutely everything in his life had been improving.

Kai felt at ease and well accepted in England. The liberal British mentality and lifestyle were to his liking, since the spirit of freedom was deeply rooted in his own temperament. *"I think that's why he liked living in England so much,"* remembers Kai's companion Kosima, who had also studied in Preston. *"I felt much the same myself – we enjoyed the international openness, the mix of different cultures and the atmosphere of tolerance."* Kai had at last found the freedom he had been seeking in vain for such a long time. He could finally do what he had wanted to do for so long. It was almost as if the motto with which we had welcomed him at the time of his birth had only now come to fulfilment:

I am awakened by the call of time
Light enshrouds me
Feelings remember
And proudly and freely consecrated to my very self
I am born into the world of humankind.

It was during his time in England that we heard Kai say for the first time, "I'm satisfied with my life and happy." This was the most beautiful and reassuring statement we ever heard from him. And he had every reason to be satisfied with his life, as he went from success

Kai at the age of 21 in England

to success. In his studies, his holiday job, his traineeship – he was showered with acclaim and praise wherever he went.

One of the traineeships that Kai undertook in the course of his studies took him to London, to the British American Tobacco corporation. He found his time in the British capital even more exciting and stimulating, and he experienced a summer month marked by professional success and happiness in his private life. The appreciation that his skills and performance met with at British American Tobacco is borne out by the reference he was given there. It reads as follows:

British American Tobacco

To whom it may concern

This letter serves to confirm that Mr Kai Thieroff, who is currently studying Law at the University of Central Lancashire, was employed by British American Tobacco as an intern from 27 July 2007 until 31 August 2007.

During this period Mr Thieroff reported to me and provided legal advice and support in respect of:

- Public International Law
- international entities such as the WHO, ISO and the OECD
- European Community Law

- European Community Consultation Processes
- The national laws of various EU Member States
- Ad hoc issues such as trade secret protection and product safety laws

The quality of Mr Thieroff's work was outstanding and he completed each assignment he was given to our fullest satisfaction.

He quickly integrated into our team and we were impressed by his willingness to learn, his analytical ability and the speed with which he completed the often very complex assignments. His thorough knowledge of information technology and resources was very helpful in finding and presenting information.

We plan to invite Mr Thieroff back for another internship next year and we would not hesitate to offer a person of his quality full-time employment should such an opportunity arise in future.

We realised just how sincerely this statement was meant when Kai's traineeship supervisor came especially from London to bid farewell to him at the memorial service we organised for our son on behalf of his family, friends and acquaintances – including many of his fellow students and friends from England. The director of PRo Publications International Ltd, the company based in Epsom south of London where Kai had worked during the semester break, was also in attendance. The company director arrived together with two female employees, who had been former colleagues of Kai's, to pay his last respects to our son. He too had been full of praise for Kai during his time at PRo Publications in the semester break. He had valued him as an absolutely reliable, conscientious and diligent employee who worked professionally and autonomously. He also stressed Kai's sociability and his capacity to hold conversations in English at a high level.

*

I did not know much about Kai's private undertakings in England. After all, he was now grown up and led his own life hundreds of kilometres away from us. But I know from what he told us that he lived his life in the company of friends – especially Kosima, one of his earliest friends, who went with him through thick and thin also during his time in England. Kosima remembers:

"When we studied together in England, Kai was an important support to me and was my best friend. It was here that our friendship was the most intense and we became acquainted with each other the most closely. When I left my boyfriend at the time amidst major drama and a lot of tears, Kai somehow helped me to emerge from these difficult weeks unscathed. He came up with something new almost every day to cheer me up. We went to the shopping centre, cooked our favourite meal together, went to a musical in Manchester, or he invited me to a wonderful bar. The way he treated me was indescribable, and I've never since experienced anything like it. For his friends, Kai made sure that nothing was impossible. Whatever happened, we always had something to laugh about; for example, we made some crazy videos – I remember performing my favourite song unbelievably

badly after three glasses of wine, and making fun of him because of his countless bottles of perfume when I cleaned his bathroom."

Always having something to laugh about – this could have been Kai's life motto at that time. I have been told that people in England especially appreciated Kai's characteristic sense of humour. He kept his friends and acquaintances entertained with his talent for imitating dialects – both English and German. With these "shows", in which his acting skills also came to the fore, he could be sure of provoking no end of laughter at social gatherings.

What else do I know about Kai's activities at that time? I remember that he liked to use the semester vacations for travel. My husband once undertook a holiday trip with him to New York, and another journey took him to Mexico. Kai's international contacts also kept him on the move during those years. He often came to Germany to visit his friends in Cologne, and he also flew to Vienna a number of times to see some friends. It was with joy and relief that I realised Kai seemed to be leading an entirely normal student life.

As Kosima's statement shows, Kai always had an ear for his friends' problems and he supported them as best he could. However, he showed this helpfulness and commitment not only towards friends and acquaintances, but occasionally also towards complete strangers, as illustrated by a touching anecdote from England around a year before Kai's death. I would like to include it here exactly as my husband wrote it down for a sad occasion – his address at Kai's memorial service:

"Kai is sitting in a McDonald's restaurant somewhere in England, munching on a hamburger. He then sees a really old but resplendently clean Morris stopping in the car park. An elderly gentleman

alights from the car, dressed in a suit that had been elegant in bygone days but by now was quite worn out, with a hat and gloves to match. The gentleman walks around the car and opens the front passenger's door for a likewise elderly lady wearing a dress that once upon a time was also very elegant but can no longer conceal its age. With an aristocratic gait, the two old-timers stride into the McDonald's restaurant and choose a table, the elderly gentleman lifts the chair back for his companion, she sits down and he also takes a seat. They are now obviously expecting a waiter to come and take their orders.

"How would we have reacted in this situation? Many of us perhaps would have hardly taken any notice: we would have been far too busy eating our own hamburgers. Some of us perhaps would have been surprised that this elderly couple did not seem to know that McDonald's is a self-service restaurant. Some of us may have sympathised with the distinguished guests and after some hesitation would have gone over to tell them that customers must get their own meals there. But surely none of us would have done what Kai did.

"Without waiting for the old people to see him sitting at his table he stands up after a brief moment, assumes the attitude of a waiter, proceeds to their table and asks the guests for their orders. They ask for his recommendations. Kai immediately makes a suggestion – something he thinks would be just right for the couple; they order it. Kai goes to the cashier, gets the desired meals, pays for them and brings them to the table where the elderly guests are sitting. While doing so, he quickly thinks of how he can justify his need to settle the bill immediately without embarrassing the distinguished guests. I have unfortunately forgotten how he did this, but I know he came up with something convincing. So he serves the elderly couple their

meals and explains to them why, to his regret, he must request immediate payment. What is the price? Kai names the sum. The elderly gentleman rummages in his wallet, only to find that he unfortunately does not have so much money with him; his companion is unable to help. 'That doesn't matter,' says Kai. 'Today, you can have your meal for whatever price you can pay.' He takes the money and thanks them politely, the old-timers thank him for the good service and the discount, and Kai returns to his hamburger and finishes his meal.

"And why did he do all this? Because he found the couple so sympathetic, so 'sweeeet', as he put it; because this image of the gleaming old car, the elderly couple that had put on their best attire for the occasion, and this misplaced visit to McDonald's deeply touched him. He of course never would have expressed it this way and certainly would have denied it, but I believe he felt something like love for these two senior citizens."

*

But then something happened that nobody would have expected – and least of all Kai himself, as we found out later: Kai, who otherwise never lost control of himself, who always saw the world through the prism of reason, had fallen in love. In late autumn 2007, when he announced that he wanted to introduce a friend to us, I realised there was a woman in Kai's life for whom he felt more than just friendship and affection. He got to know her on a visit to Cologne. She was also highly gifted, he told us, and with her he could for the first time ever conduct good, deep conversations – conversations at eye level. I only saw the two of them together once, when we invited them to a restaurant. I still remember how lovingly Kai looked after the young woman, who had a headache that evening, and anticipated her every wish. I knew right there and then that Kai had fallen in love. It was not at all clear for me, however, with what intensity the storm of emotions was raging within him.

We only learnt this after his death, in a letter he had written to his lover shortly after Christmas that we found in his flat in Preston. Kai had not told us much about his beloved one. It was only through this letter that we understood that Kai was madly in love – in a way that was not only entirely new to him, but that he had been convinced was not even possible. In this letter he attempted to explain to the young woman, and to himself, what had happened:

"I have never really understood people in love, especially men. I always dismissed this as exaggeratedly irrational, emotional prattle and had actually assumed that above a certain level of intelligence one can no longer fall in love, since one must then be aware of the entire substitutability. But I only saw things this way because at least theoretically, I could have imagined (…) substituting anyone in the world. Until I met you!"

And Kai, my sensitive son who never did things by halves, especially in matters of the heart, put everything into question as a result of this new experience of being in love:

"Up until now I have been quite happy and contented in my life. And a girl has suddenly come into my life who is turning everything upside down, and all at once it has become clear to me that I was living in an illusion of happiness. (...) Throughout my life, I have (...) never been so completely contented and happy to be alive as when you are lying in my arms."

Kai had to make the painful experience that his newly found happiness also entailed a great danger: loss of self-determination. He had largely determined the course of his own life from the outset. Even as a child he had decided for himself who would number among his friends, and he later also decided for himself in favour of the school in Cologne, legal studies and living in England. By the end of his schooldays at the latest, he had been leading his own life entirely – and now no longer had it under his control. He understood that dependence was likewise a part of his new world of emotions – dependence on the affection of his loved one. He wrote in that letter:

"Unfortunately, this wonderful present you have given me is also accompanied by path of suffering, which I hope will be transformed into a pathway to heaven before it leads me to hell, and that we can come together to be happy together."

The letter ends with the words:

"I implore you to give us a chance."

Kai's supplication was not answered, however; this chance was not granted to him. His path of suffering was not transformed into a pathway to heaven but in fact did lead to hell – a hell of emotional torment from which Kai liberated himself by dropping an unexpected bombshell.

A conscious decision

For us the disaster came out of the blue, at a time we had least been expecting it – at a time when we believed the gloom accompanying the end of Kai's schooldays and the despondency that had taken hold of him in ninth grade had been overcome. Kai seemed to us to be more stable and well-balanced than ever before in his life, and he had some major plans: within only a few weeks of obtaining his Bachelor's degree, he intended to begin a traineeship with the German embassy in Bangkok. He then planned to undertake a Master's degree and a further course in American law and finally go to London or New York. Nothing more seemed to be standing in the way of a brilliant legal career.

I had my first inkling of the approaching catastrophe on a warm, sunny afternoon in early May 2008. I had been trying to contact Kai by phone for several hours, but in vain – he did not answer his mobile phone. As the mother of an adult son I knew that this in itself should be no cause for concern, but my unrest grew with each further hour that Kai could not be reached, and I was overcome by despair. In the two and a half years that Kai had now already been living in England we spoke to each other every day, and he had never ignored my calls for such a long time.

My foreboding that something had happened was confirmed when the police called the next day. A black Fiat Punto, registered in my husband's name, had been found abandoned on the Scottish coast. The key still was in the ignition, and there was an empty bottle of schnapps in the car. The world caved in over me: although in principle several scenarios were possible – that Kai had wanted to be alone in his pain, or he had had an accident – I knew Kai had done himself harm. The alcohol was a merciful ally for him, because it clouded his thinking and thus enabled him to carry out his plan.

I felt a surge of panic, and as it abated the pain set in. Pain that grew to immense proportions when the police informed us that a letter addressed to us parents had been found in Kai's flat. Kai had informed us of his departure on a computer printout with his signature:

Dear parents,
Right now, you'll be devastated and you won't understand why I have done this. I don't want to justify it at all or apologise, because it's inexcusable. I just want to let you know that I love you more than anything in the world and that it was you who stopped me from taking this step for so many years. But I can now no longer remain alive just for others when I myself don't see any sense overall in continuing. I don't want to enter into my motivation here, but I can say this much: for me, the world isn't worth living in if there's a painless alternative – and there is one. I love you. Please try to come to terms with my action.

Your Kai

Three long weeks between hope and despair then followed. Perhaps Kai had not carried out his plan after all; perhaps he had gone into hiding somewhere unknown to us and would greet us safe and sound, healed from his emotional confusion, in just a few days' time. The worst part was the uncertainty, but we simply had to keep waiting.

Meanwhile, the search for Kai was in full swing in England and Scotland. A land and water search involving the coastguard and a rescue helicopter was started in the area of the coast where his car had been found. But there was still no trace of Kai. The Preston police issued an urgent request among the town's university students to help in the search. Whoever had information about his whereabouts or his plans was to contact the police in Preston. They informed the press that there was cause for great concern, because Kai's disappearance was out of character and his family in Germany was extremely worried. But nobody could help, and the appeal launched by Kai's friends on the Internet also remained unanswered.

The spark of hope that we had been keeping alive was extinguished one day in late May. A telephone call from the police confirmed all our fears. Kai's body had been washed up in the Kyle of Tongue, a bay in the far north of the Scottish Highlands. His lifeless body bore a rucksack weighed down with dumbbells.

My son, who had never done things by halves, also wanted to leave nothing to chance when he went into the water.

*

Intense darkness settled over me and held me in its grasp for weeks and months on end. The uncertainty as to Kai's whereabouts was harsh, but the certainty of his death was a thousand times worse. Kai had been my only child, and my loss as a mother was one hundred per cent.

I saw the world around me as through a veil: the police officers who went through our flat to gather DNA samples from Kai's toothbrush and hairbrush for identification; then our journey to Preston with some friends of Kai's to clear out his flat. And then finding the letter in Kai's flat to the young woman he had loved, the letter that finally gave us a clue as to his motivation for this act. Added to this were the many telephone calls from the police with more and more new details, and later the calls from the crematorium: it was as if Kai were dying over and over again. But what we desired the most – to bid farewell to our child in a quiet moment – was not possible amidst the restlessness of those days. It was only with the dignified memorial service we held on a larger scale some weeks after Kai's death, and later the urn burial in a close circle of family and friends, that brought us the peace in our thoughts that we had been longing for, and we could finally bid farewell to our son.

*

I wish Kai could have explained the reasons for his fateful decision more clearly, but this was not to be. Rather, the leitmotif of his earlier times of crisis came to the fore once more in his farewell letter: the senselessness which he had felt time and again and which had gnawed on his enjoyment of life. It had broken out once again and finally brought him to his knees.

I am convinced today that Kai's final, disastrous crisis was triggered by his experience of love, by his intense feelings which had apparently remained unanswered. But it was probably not this alone. The emotions that raged within him also brought something more to the surface of his consciousness, something no less fateful: the weltschmerz that had always latently plagued him and against which he was finally defenceless.

Kai wrote on his Facebook profile of how he had dealt with this pain in day-to-day life and how he had come to terms with the baseness of this world in general: *Cynicism is my armour, sarcasm my sword and irony my shield* was one of his favourite quotes that he posted there. I still remember how happy and excited he was when he discovered this sentence, with which he could identify so well. And it was true: with cynicism, sarcasm and irony he armed himself against all the evil that he saw and experienced in this world, and they afforded him protection. But now that his outlook on the world had started to falter in view of the storm of emotions that had taken hold of him, this strategy had failed: his armour of cynicism had become riddled with holes, his sword of sarcasm was blunt and his shield of irony was broken. The last website that Kai called up on his computer was that of Austrian Television – a report about a man who had held his own daughter prisoner in his cellar for a quarter of a century and repeatedly raped her and fathered six children with her during that time. I think this was also something Kai could no longer bear. The pain of his own situation blended with his newly experienced pain in light of the condition of the world and forced him to act.

To this day, I derive support and comfort from the fact that Kai made the conscious decision to leave this world of his own free will.

In dubio pro libertate – when in doubt, for freedom – was a further motto on his Facebook account. And freedom for him also meant freedom to decide – namely in favour of suicide, in German also referred to as "free death", his "painless alternative". He had thus regained his freedom to make his own decisions, which he had momentarily lost in the frenzy of love, and he left this world *proudly and freely consecrated to his very self.*

*

After Kai's death we received numerous letters of condolence; these were a genuine help and support to me at that difficult time. I was overwhelmed to learn how many people, even strangers, shared our pain and offered us their assistance. In early June 2008, only a few days after our fears had been confirmed, we received a very personal letter of condolence from the Lancashire Law School in Preston, in which a lecturer and member of the Board of Directors gave testimony to Kai's personality on behalf of all staff and students from the Law School and expressed to us in warm words her commiserations in view of our great loss. As documentation of the widespread sympathy shown towards us after Kai's death, I quote this letter:

4th June 2008

Dear Dr and Mrs Thieroff,

On behalf of everyone in the Law School, I wanted to write to say how desperately sorry we all are to learn of the tragic events that have emerged about Kai this week. There are no words that can adequately express the deep sadness and shock of this news. Our thoughts and sympathies are with you both and Kai's extended family and friends at this dreadful time. We cannot begin to comprehend the devastation and anguish that you must be feeling.

I am sure there is nothing that can lessen your pain at the moment, but I do hope that over time you will be able to gain some comfort from knowing that Kai was held in the very highest regard by everyone who knew him. All of his tutors have described him as an outstanding student, sometimes the best in the subject, who dedicated himself to his studies. He was a most likeable and confident young man who impressed all who met him. He was polite, considerate, and mature. Among his peers, he was looked up to as something of a natural leader, a model student who seemed to have such a promising future.

When I sat in with members of the teaching team in their discussions with the police, each tutor quite spontaneously painted the same picture of Kai. There were glowing accounts of his performance and attitude, a bright and popular student who set and maintained high standards. His friends spoke of their utmost respect and liking for Kai. There was disbelief that anything could have happened along with hope that he would be found safe and well.

The staff and students have found it so difficult to understand what has happened. It must be an impossible time for you. Please take strength from knowing that in everything he did in his University life, Kai was a young man of whom you can both be immensely proud. Whatever happened in the final moments of his life, he was an outstanding person who contributed much in his short life and will be remembered by us all in the Law School with great fondness and affection.

I am so very, very sorry.

*

At the end of this book I would like to quote the renowned talent researcher Prof. Franz J. Mönks. It was during the establishment of my Children's College that I first met and came to admire Prof. Mönks, who was active at the University of Nijmegen in the Netherlands and is regarded as one of the fathers of European talent research. He has generously provided me with advice and assistance ever since the early days of my activities for the promotion of giftedness. Kai was often present in the afternoons and evenings when we discussed the Children's College, so that Prof. Mönks had ample opportunity to talk with him, observe him and get to know him as a person. He writes of Kai:

From the outset, Kai showed great interest in everything that was going on around him. The range of interests that he already showed as a baby was extraordinary. He could already read at the age of four, and by the time he started school when he was five, not even difficult texts were any hindrance to him. Not only his reading competence, but also his language skills were well beyond the standard of other children of his age, and he was far ahead of them in terms of intellectual development. His behaviour was marked by curiosity and a desire to learn.

His school admission marked the beginning of a time of suffering for this bright and cognitively boisterous young boy. Boredom undermined and destroyed his wide-awake intellect. His motivation to learn rapidly declined. And by the time he left school at the age of fourteen, his marks had reached a low point. From today's perspective, it can be stated that the teaching staff were completely unable to cope with the situation. Such an inquisitive child with such a thirst for knowledge was a far cry from the average level of talent for which teachers are normally trained. Hermann Hesse aptly describes this situation in his novel Beneath the Wheel *(1906): "A schoolmaster would rather have a number of donkeys in his class than one genius."*

Kai was an astute and independent thinker, always amiable and courteous in his demeanour. He was delicate and highly sensitive. According to Dabrowski, this high degree of sensitivity is a salient characteristic of positive disintegration and thus the driving force of a person's individual development. High sensitivity is eminently significant particularly among highly gifted people, because they experience all the more intensely the inner conflicts between "that which is" and "that which should be". The positive processing of this conflict borne by emotional sensitivity, according to Dabrowski, opens the door to the development of one's personality at the highest level.

Kai forthrightly went his own way as a highly gifted and highly sensitive person.

*

Indeed, Kai forthrightly went his own way – to the bitter end, which he saw as the only logical choice. Even though he left us by doing so, and left us with an emptiness in our hearts that can never be filled, I have learnt to accept his decision. I am grateful for the many beautiful and special moments we had with him, and I can say today with a sincere heart that I have made my peace with this situation.

Epilogue

For a long time after Kai's suicide, I wondered time and again what blame I was to bear as a mother – or we as an entire family – for the fact that our son did not find his life sufficiently worth living. What could we have done differently, or better, in accompanying Kai? I have not found an answer to this question in all the years that have passed since that time. I still believe we did everything within our power for Kai. But this was apparently not enough. The task was too great for us as a family to handle alone.

Sometimes I wonder whether Kai would have decided differently if he had been more emotionally stable, if he had not suffered so many setbacks in his life – and especially in his school career. I remember Kai's cheerful disposition at the time of the Children's Club and his inner balance during his student days in England, and I am convinced that in these phases of his life it was his environment – an environment of respect, acceptance and self-confidence – that allowed him to flourish. But this is exactly what was lacking throughout a major portion of his school days, and the feeling of not being fully accepted as a person eroded his self-respect and heightened his already extreme vulnerability.

Today, I think children like Kai can only have a real chance in life with a concerted effort on the part of the whole of society. This above all entails eliminating prejudices towards gifted children and adolescents. I hope that by telling Kai's story I have managed to show that gifted young people are by no means the socially incompetent high-flyers they are often seen to be; that when they disassociate themselves from their classmates and teachers at school, this is not normally due to arrogance but because they feel misunderstood or unjustly treated; that for many of them a successful school career is by no means guaranteed despite their high level of intelligence and performance, but rather that gaining school leaving qualification requires an enormous feat of strength on the part of their families. For these children, the necessity to adapt intellectually to their environment and dampen their exuberant creativity is so tormenting that they withdraw into their "shells" – as a purely self-protective measure – and refuse to participate at school. Society and politics are called upon here to provide appropriate schooling for these children too.

With this book I would like to give encouragement to the parents of gifted "problem children" whose daughters or sons give them no end of concern. Despite its tragedy, Kai's story demonstrates one thing above all: that it is worth the effort to fight for these children; that even early school leavers can be newly motivated as long as their parents are prepared to act as intermediaries "between the worlds" and to sound out compromises that are acceptable to their children.

Such families can only be relieved of this immense responsibility through the solidarity of society as a whole. This will bear its own rewards, since gifted young people ultimately have great intellectual and creative potential in store for society. We must together ensure that these young people are not left behind in their educational careers and that they are not crushed under the pain they bear within themselves – the pain of being different.